THE VENETIAN TWINS
(I due gemelli Veneziani)

By
CARLO GOLDONI

Translated by
MICHAEL FEINGOLD

SAMUEL FRENCH, INC.

45 West 25th Street
NEW YORK 10010
LONDON

7623 Sunset Boulevard
HOLLYWOOD 90046
TORONTO

Copyright © 2002 by Michael Feingold

ALL RIGHTS RESERVED

CAUTION: Professionals and amateurs are hereby warned that THE VENETIAN TWINS is subject to a royalty. It is fully protected under the copyright laws of the United States of America, the British Commonwealth, including Canada, and all other countries of the Copyright Union. All rights, including professional, amateur, motion pictures, recitation, lecturing, public reading, radio broadcasting, television, and the rights of translation into foreign languages are strictly reserved. In its present form the play is dedicated to the reading public only.

The amateur live stage performance rights to THE VENETIAN TWINS are controlled exclusively by Samuel French, Inc. and royalty arrangements and licenses must be secured well in advance of presentation. PLEASE NOTE that amateur royalty fees are set upon application in accordance with your producing circumstances. When applying for a royalty quotation and license please give us the number of performances intended, dates of production, your seating capacity and admission fee. Royalties are payable one week before the opening performance of the play to Samuel French, Inc., at 45 West 25th Street, New York, NY 10010; or at 7623 Sunset Blvd., Hollywood, CA 90046, or to Samuel French (Canada), Ltd., 100 Lombard Street, Toronto, Ontario, Canada M5C 1M3.

Royalty of the required amount must be paid whether the play is presented for charity or gain and whether or not admission is charged.

Stock royalty quoted on application to Samuel French, Inc.

For all other rights than those stipulated above, apply to Mitch Douglas, ICM, 40 West 57th Street, New York, New York 10019

Particular emphasis is laid on the question of amateur or professional readings, permission and terms for which must be secured in writing from Samuel French, Inc.

Copying from this book in whole or in part is strictly forbidden by law, and the right of performance is not transferable.

Whenever the play is produced the following notice must appear on all programs, printing and advertising for the play: "Produced by special arrangement with Samuel French, Inc."

Due authorship credit must be given on all programs, printing and advertising for the play.

ISBN 0 573 62763 0   Printed In Hong Kong by YTL   #24014

No one shall commit or authorize any act or omission by which the copyright of, or the right to copyright, this play may be impaired.

No one shall make any changes in this play for the purpose of production.

Publication of this play does not imply availability for performance. Both amateurs and professionals considering a production are *strongly* advised in their own interests to apply to Samuel French, Inc., for written permission before starting rehearsals, advertising, or booking a theatre.

No part of this book may be reproduced, stored in a retrieval system, or transmitted in any form, by any means, now known or yet to be invented, including mechanical, electronic, photocopying, recording, videotaping, or otherwise, without the prior written permission of the publisher.

IMPORTANT BILLING AND CREDIT REQUIREMENTS

All producers of THE VENETIAN TWINS *must* give credit to the Author and the Translator of the Play all programs distributed in connection with performances of the Play and in all instances in which the title of the Play appears for purposes of advertising, publicizing or otherwise exploiting the Play and/or a production. The names *must* appear on separate lines, one which no other name appears, immediately following the title, and *must* appear in size of type not less than fifty percent the size of the title type. Billing should appear as follows:

THE VENETIAN TWINS
(I due gemelli Veneziani)

By CARLO GOLDONI

Translated by MICHAEL FEINGOLD

In addition, the following credit must appear in all programs distributed in connection with performances of the play:

THE VENETIAN TWINS
was commissioned and first produced by the
Pearl Theatre Company, New York City.

This translation of THE VENETIAN TWINS was first produced by the Pearl Theatre Company at Theatre 80 St. Marks, New York City, where it received its first performance on December 16, 1994. It was directed by John Rando, with the following cast:

ROSAURA	Rachel Botchan
COLOMBINA	Robin Leslie Brown
PROFESSOR BALANZONI	John Wylie
BRIGHELLA	Greg Steinbruner
ZANETTO	Arnie Burton
PANCRAZIO	Clement Fowler
BEATRICE	Jennifer Thomas
FLORINDO	Michael James Reed
LELIO	Kevin Black
TONINO	Arnie Burton
ARLECCHINO	Mace Perlman
PORTER	Bradford Cover
TIBURZIO	John Wylie
CONSTABLE	Bradford Cover

Music by Thomas Cabaniss

Sets by Robert Joel Schwartz

Lighting by Stephen Petrilli

Costumes by Deborah Rooney

Masks by Renzo Antonello

Production Stage Manager — Lynn Bogarde

CHARACTERS

PROFESSOR BALANZONI, a lawyer from Bologna

ROSAURA, thought to be his daughter

PANCRAZIO, the Professor's friend and houseguest

ZANETTO, the silly twin*

TONINO, the clever twin*

LELIO, the Professor's nephew

BEATRICE, Tonino's lover

FLORINDO, Tonino's friend

COLOMBINA and BRIGHELLA, servants in the Professor's house

ARLECCHINO, Zanetto's servant

TIBURZIO, a goldsmith

A CONSTABLE

GUARDS**
SERVANTS**

*played by one actor
**Guards and servants were omitted in the Pearl Theatre production. These and other omissions are indicated by brackets [ ] in the text.

SCENE

Verona

This translation was originally commissioned and performed
by the Pearl Theatre Company, New York City.

TRANSLATOR'S NOTE

With some minor modifications, this is an accurate translation of *I due gemelli Veneziani* as published in the standard Italian edition of Goldoni's collected works — the only extant English version, as far as I know, that comes within shouting distance of the original. However, John Rando's production was so ingenious, in the many ways it brought vitality to this 250-year-old play, that it seemed unfair for other theatres not to have at least a few glimpses into possible ways of "stretching" the script. Accordingly, in this text I have allowed some of his directorial business to seep into what are otherwise Goldoni's stage directions. Lines that we cut in the Pearl performance — the 18th century had its wordy side — are enclosed in brackets.

John wanted this transitional play to have at least a slight flavor of the brawling, town-square style of *commedia* performance, occasionally spilling over into audience interactions, that Goldoni was fighting to eradicate. I stood by and let it happen, partly because evoking the spirit of the era seemed as important to me as the words, but mostly because I knew I could trust John not to bury the play in pointless or tiresome improvisational shenanigans. Thanks to his discretion, and the inventiveness of some lively young comic actors, the results more than justified my trust. It would have been impossible to load down a published script with all of these amusing frills, but I have found space for one or two of the better bits.

The masked characters in the Pearl production were the servants Brighella and Arlecchino, traditionally the low comics or *zanni*. This doesn't exactly accord with Goldoni's script, in which Brighella is a very specific sketch of an old retainer, and Arlecchino a very specifically put-upon, extravagant figure. Goldoni himself wanted to do away with masks altogether; one of his great victories was persuading the actor who created the dual roles of Tonino and Zanetto to play them unmasked. But the masks our *zanni* wore, created by Renzo Antonello, master maskmaker of Vicenza, added a layer of beauty and mystery that the young actors performing the roles could never have supplied barefaced. It may not have been accurate, but it was powerful. Anyone who has worked with masks knows that they can create stunning effects. Rather than echo Goldoni's stringency, I would say: If you use them in this play, use them sparingly and wisely, remembering that he would have preferred none at all.

At the Pearl, the masked figures, with Colombina added, were used to open and close the play with a dance, and to change the set between scenes; the two men also appeared masked miming an accompaniment to Zanetto's serenade. I haven't included any of this in the stage directions, since every set designer will find a different solution for the play's interior-exterior shift, and every director will have a different view of the play's tone and how to frame it.

Michael Feinglod

This translation is dedicated first of all to D.P., my own personal Tonino/Zanetto; and secondarily to John, Robin, the tireless Lynn, the indefatigable Arnie, and to John Wylie, the world's tallest Dottore and shortest Tiburzio.

ACT I

Scene 1

(ROSAURA's room.
ROSAURA at dressing table, curling tongs in her hair, facing imaginary mirror downstage. COLOMBINA shoves her aside to get at mirror.)

ROSAURA. Colombina dear, don't you think you should finish doing my hair before you start fixing your own? *(Pushes her away from mirror.)*

COLOMBINA. Miss, I've been working on your hair for two hours, teasing, waving, curling. But you're never satisfied; you keep mussing it up with your fingers till I don't know what to do about it.

ROSAURA. How dare you say that! You've left mine in this horrible mess while you waste time fiddling with yours.

COLOMBINA. Well, really, you're not the only one here with hair on her head, you know.

ROSAURA. Yes, but I'm the mistress and you're the maid.

COLOMBINA. Thanks, you don't have to remind me.

ROSAURA. Now finish this up. My prospective fiancé will be here any minute; I don't want him to see me like this.

(They jostle for position at mirror.)

COLOMBINA. *(Picking up hand mirror.)* Mine's on his way too, Miss, and I want to look my best.

ROSAURA. *(Getting up from her place at mirror)* What? Do you think you're as good as me, you conceited little —

COLOMBINA. Don't you talk to me like that, Miss. Show some respect if you know what's good for you. *(Sits in chair ROSAURA has just vacated.)*

ROSAURA. *(Slapping her.)* You rude thing! Get up and get to work, before I beat you black and blue.

COLOMBINA. *(Getting up.)* God in Heaven! *You'll* beat *me*?

ROSAURA. Talking back to your mistress like that? I'll tell my father, you slut.

COLOMBINA. *(Expostulating to audience.)* What a mistress! And what a father! But don't worry, I know how to deal with *him*.

ROSAURA. *(Sitting back down at dressing table.)* And just what do you mean by that, you little sneak?

COLOMBINA. Stop it, stop all these insults, or I'll lose my temper and say something I shouldn't, you know?

ROSAURA. Go on, say it, what are you going to say, you liar?

COLOMBINA. I could say you're ...

ROSAURA. *(Armed with curling tongs.)* Yes?

COLOMBINA. Never mind; I've kept quiet this long, but I may not want to much longer.

(The PROFESSOR comes in.)

PROFESSOR. What's all this noise? What happened? What's going on?

ROSAURA. Oh, father! Punish this beast. She insults me and hurts me and has no respect for me at all.

PROFESSOR. *(To COLOMBINA.)* What? Is that a way to treat my little girl?

COLOMBINA. Don't think you can stop me, sir. My mother told me everything, you know?

PROFESSOR. *(Aside.)* Damn that woman and her big mouth! If she were still alive I'd whip her to death. *(Taking COLOMBINA aside, softly.)* For the love of God, Colombina, don't say anything about all that. I'll make it worth your while, I promise.

COLOMBINA. *(Softly to PROFESSOR.)* Oh, right, I should just stand here and let her insult me.

ROSAURA. *(Running to PROFESSOR and trying to pull him away from COLOMBINA.)* Really, father —

PROFESSOR. *(Gabbling, pushing ROSAURA behind screen to dress.)* Come, come, no time to worry about all that, you've got to be

THE VENETIAN TWINS

ready for your fiancé, Zanetto Bisognosi. His father was the famous Venetian banker Pantalone, though he was really brought up in Bergamo by his uncle Stefano, who's one of the richest men in Lombardy.

COLOMBINA. *(As she helps ROSAURA.)* And don't forget that I'm supposed to get married too, to his valet. You promised.

PROFESSOR. *(Softly to COLOMBINA, pulling her out from behind screen.)* Yes, yes, we'll do it, you'll be happy — as long as you keep quiet!

COLOMBINA. Fine, if you want me to keep quiet, a husband is the best way to stop my mouth.

PROFESSOR. By the way, Rosaura, have you seen Signor Pancrazio lately?

ROSAURA. Oh, yes, I see him all the time.

PROFESSOR. What a charming man he is!

ROSAURA. Oh, yes, always so full of good advice for me.

PROFESSOR. As long as I live, he'll be welcome in this house.

ROSAURA. That's fine. He's so nice and helpful.

COLOMBINA. Well, if you don't mind my saying so, I think he's a complete crook.

PROFESSOR. Hold your nasty tongue. Why would you want to say such a spiteful thing?

COLOMBINA. I know what I'm talking about. Let's leave it at that.

BRIGHELLA. *(Coming in.)* Signor Perfessor, Miss ma'am, this Signor Zanetto from Bergamo just got here; he's at the door getting off his horse and talking to his groom.

PROFESSOR. Thank God he got here. Daughter mine, I'll go receive him in person, and bring him right up here to meet you.

(The PROFESSOR goes out.)

ROSAURA. Brighella, tell me, you saw Signor Zanetto, what's he like? Is he handsome? Is he refined?

BRIGHELLA. Well, Miss ma'am, I'll tell you, as for handsome, he ain't too bad, he's young and he'll get by; but far as I can tell, there ain't much goin' on upstairs. He didn't even know which side of the horse to get down from. Funny, his face is the spit and image of his twin brother Tonino's, who I used to see all the time when I lived in Venice. But I'll tell you, the face may be the same, but the rest couldn't be more different, 'cause the other one's a clever, dashin' kind of fella, while this one's dumb as a post and twice as stiff.

ROSAURA. I don't like what you're telling me at all.

COLOMBINA. *(To BRIGHELLA.)* Signor Zanetto has a valet named Arlecchino, did he come with him?

BRIGHELLA. He ain't here yet, he's comin' with his master's luggage.

COLOMBINA. Too bad. I can't wait to see him.

BRIGHELLA. I know, I know, he's gonna be your one and lonely.

COLOMBINA. What are you, jealous? Drop dead.

(COLOMBINA goes out.)

ROSAURA. Brighella, tell me, how did you come to know this family in Venice? And just why was Signor Zanetto brought up in Bergamo?

BRIGHELLA. I used to work for this really rich businessman in Venice, and his best friend was Signor Pantalone Bisognosi, who had these twin sons. And besides them Signor Pantalone had a daughter, and he sent her off to Bergamo, to this brother of his, I think his name was Stefanello, who was rich and had no kids, but before that he'd already sent her older brother, Signor Zanetto, there. And what I heard, hanging around their house, was that the daughter got lost somehow, that she never got to Bergamo. She disappeared along the way and they could never find out what happened. And that's all I know about them, except that the Bisognosi family had this great big fancy house on the Piazza, and everybody thought he was the richest man in Venice.

(Leaning confidentially toward ROSAURA, he holds out his hand. She puts a coin in it. He waits for another, sees it isn't coming, pockets the first.)

ROSAURA. Well, I suppose it's all right, but I'm sorry Signor Zanetto isn't as clever as his brother.

THE VENETIAN TWINS

BRIGHELLA. Well, here he comes with the master. Now you can look him over and see if I'm not telling the truth.

(BRIGHELLA goes out. The PROFESSOR comes in with ZANETTO.)

ROSAURA. *(Aside.)* I like his face. Maybe he's not as big a fool as Brighella says.

PROFESSOR. *(Struggling to hold down the nervous ZANETTO.)* Come in, come in, don't stand on ceremony here. Daughter darling, here's Signor Zanetto.

ZANETTO. *(Presenting wilted bouquet.)* Miss fiancée, I'm glad to meet you.

ROSAURA. I'm your humble servant, Signor Zanetto.

ZANETTO. *(Aside, withdrawing bouquet.)* Oh, it's only the servant. Pretty girl! *(To PROFESSOR.)* So tell me, sir, where's the lucky fiancée?

PROFESSOR. Right here. This is my daughter, the girl you're going to marry.

ZANETTO. But she just told me she was the servant girl.

PROFESSOR. Oh, no, she said she was your humble servant, just as a compliment, out of politeness.

ZANETTO. I see; but that's no way to start.

PROFESSOR. Why not?

ZANETTO. Because I don't think in a marriage you should have any lies or politeness.

ROSAURA. *(Aside.)* He really is a fool; even so, I think I like him.

PROFESSOR. Really, you mustn't let it worry you.

ROSAURA. Believe me, Signor Zanetto, I'm totally sincere, I would never lie to anyone, and I have the highest respect and admiration for you.

ZANETTO. A lot of good that does me.

ROSAURA. Perhaps you don't like the way I phrase myself?

ZANETTO. Oh, Miss, you can phrase yourself any way you like.

ROSAURA. Or perhaps my looks don't appeal to you?

ZANETTO. Never mind all that. I've come to Verona to get married; I'm just waiting for Arlecchino to get here with my clothes, and the jewels and money.

ROSAURA. Fine, but aren't you going to marry me?

ZANETTO. What good is all this fancy talk? Let's just shake hands and call it a deal.

ROSAURA. *(Aside.)* What an odd duck he is!

PROFESSOR. But dear son-in-law, you can't get married just like that. You must say a few words to your fiancée, something charming or affectionate.

ZANETTO. *(To PROFESSOR.)* Yes, you're right. *(To ROSAURA, kneeling.)* I'm yours, only yours. I adore your pretty little face. I want to — *(To PROFESSOR.)* Father-in-law, do me a favor.

PROFESSOR. What is it?

ZANETTO. Get out of here. You make me nervous.

PROFESSOR. Only too glad to oblige. I would never stand in your way. *(Softly to ROSAURA.)* Daughter dear, be discreet. He's a bit of a fool, but he's filthy rich. *(To ZANETTO.)* Till later, son-in-law. *(Aside.)* When Fate sends money, smile at the messenger.

(The PROFESSOR goes out.)

ZANETTO. *(To PROFESSOR, as he goes.)* Yours, signor. *(To ROSAURA.)* So, Miss fiancée, we're going to be man and wife.

ROSAURA. I hope so.

ZANETTO. And we just stand here like a couple of sticks?

ROSAURA. Well, what do you think we should do?

ZANETTO. Oh, come on! Man and wife.

ROSAURA. Man and wife is what we're going to be — I'll say it again, I hope so — but we're not married yet.

ZANETTO. No? Well, what do we have to do to get married?

ROSAURA. We have to go through a whole long ceremony.

ZANETTO. Let's cut it short. Do you want me to be your husband?

ROSAURA. Yes, dear Zanetto, very much.

ZANETTO. Good, and I want you to be my wife. So what other ceremony do we need? This is the sweetest ceremony in the world.

ROSAURA. Very well said. But we don't do things that way here.

ZANETTO. No? Then I'm going back to Bergamo. Back to the

THE VENETIAN TWINS 15

mountains, where I grew up. There we just do it when we want to. A couple of words and we're married, and that's all the ceremony a man and his wife ever get.

ROSAURA. Well, I repeat, here we have a solemn ritual.

ZANETTO. But how long does the ritual take?

ROSAURA. It goes on at least two days.

ZANETTO. What, you think I can wait that long?

ROSAURA. You're in an awful hurry.

ZANETTO. We do it right now or not at all.

ROSAURA. But that would be a terrible insult to me.

ZANETTO. What kind of insult is it to get married? I know a lot of girls who'd love to be insulted that way.

ROSAURA. But really! Can't you wait even one day?

ZANETTO. But sweetness, why can't we have these rituals and ceremonies after we're married? Let's get the marriage going right now; after that we can do the ceremonying for a whole year and I won't mind.

ROSAURA. Really, Signor Zanetto, I think you're making fun of me.

ZANETTO. Oh, no, I want to make fun with you.

ROSAURA. All in good time.

ZANETTO. You know what they say: The best time is right now. Come on, don't make me wait any longer.

(He comes to her and tries to grab her hand.)

    ROSAURA. Stop that!
    ZANETTO. What for?
    ROSAURA. I told you, behave.
    ZANETTO. This is how I behave.

(He tries to embrace her; she slaps him.)

ROSAURA. Rude thing! *(ZANETTO, astonished, stands stock still, touching his hand to his cheek. Staring straight at ROSAURA, he makes the motion of the slap, bows to her, and runs out without saying a word.)* God in Heaven! What a vulgar man! How could he be so coarse? [I never would have believed it; at first glance he only seemed

16   **THE VENETIAN TWINS**

a little foolish. But it shows you that looks are deceiving — even a wolf can wear sheep's clothing.] It's not safe for a woman to be left alone with any man. There's always some danger in it. Dear Signor Pancrazio has told me so time and again — Oh, but there he is. Really, just one look at his face and you can tell what a good heart he has.

PANCRAZIO. *(Entering.)* Heaven bless you, child. What's wrong? You look upset.

ROSAURA. Oh, Signor Pancrazio, if you knew what I've just been through!

PANCRAZIO. Dear, dear! Go on, tell me everything. You know you can trust me.

ROSAURA. I will tell you. You know that my father's arranged for me to marry this man from Venice.

PANCRAZIO. *(Aside.)* I wish I didn't know it!

ROSAURA. Well, he just got here today, coming from Bergamo.

PANCRAZIO. *(Aside.)* Pity he didn't break his neck on the road!

ROSAURA. And it turns out that he's a bit of a fool, and also horribly rude.

PANCRAZIO. What else can you expect from a fool?

ROSAURA. My father insisted on my meeting him right away.

PANCRAZIO. That's bad.

ROSAURA. And then he left me alone with the man.

PANCRAZIO. That's worse.

ROSAURA. And then —

PANCRAZIO. I can only imagine!

ROSAURA. He said all these coarse things to me —

PANCRAZIO. All very clever, I suppose?

ROSAURA. Oh, yes.

PANCRAZIO. And did he do any coarse things?

ROSAURA. He did.

PANCRAZIO. Well, go on; what happened then?

ROSAURA. He was so rude I had to slap him.

PANCRAZIO. Oh, brava, you clever girl, you perfect child! You should be listed among the great women of this century. [I can't find enough words to praise the brilliant way you chose to act!] That's exactly the way to treat such men; if that's how they treat a woman, humiliate them. Oh, let me kiss the noble hand, the glorious hand that did the deed! A little kiss to show my reverence and admiration for a

THE VENETIAN TWINS

hand the whole world should applaud.

(He takes her hand and kisses it tenderly. The kisses get sloppier until she snatches it away, puzzled.)

ROSAURA. Are you really so proud of me just because I lost my temper?

PANCRAZIO. [But just think!] You did the perfect thing! Nowadays it isn't easy to find a young woman modest enough to slap her suitor's face. Keep at it, keep practicing this lovely habit. Get used to suspecting the worst from these young men, who will only betray you or abuse you. If your heart does find itself longing for love, look for a lover who is worthy of you.

ROSAURA. But where should I look?

PANCRAZIO. Oh, Rosaura, I'm not in a position right now to say anything more about that. But I think of you and what's good for you more often than you imagine. Enough of that. Someday you'll understand.

ROSAURA. Signor Pancrazio, I know how good and kind you are. [You're so eager to help us out here that we'd never dream of asking you for any more favors.] So I feel I must tell you the truth: I don't dislike Signor Zanetto at all, and if he only had a little more self-control, well, maybe … who knows ...

PANCRAZIO. Oh, no! Oh, no! Bite your tongue! [Your purity has made you do a great thing; don't ruin it with these disgusting emotions.] No, how could you choose someone so revolting for a lover? A man with no sense of shame has no right to come anywhere near you. You've proved that you deserve someone much better. [Don't ever even mention his name in my presence again.]

ROSAURA. You're right, Signor Pancrazio. I'm sorry; it was just a moment of weakness. I'll tell my father I don't want to marry him.

PANCRAZIO. Brava! Now that's what I like to hear. When you talk to your father, I'll back you up.

ROSAURA. Thank you. I'll need your help. *(Aside.)* He is so kind, and so smart! My father's lucky to have him for a friend! And I'm lucky to have his good advice!

(ROSAURA goes out.)

PANCRAZIO. *(Alone.)* If my fake honesty and my false good advice don't get me Rosaura, there's no hope, because I'm not young, good-looking, or rich. But maybe, who knows, my trickery will get me what I want. These days, if you know how to lie, you know how to live, and the smarter you pretend to be, the smarter you are.

(PANCRAZIO goes out.)

Scene 2

*(Street.
BEATRICE arrives with FLORINDO, [attended by a SERVANT].)*

BEATRICE. Signor Florindo, I simply must go back to Venice.
FLORINDO. Now? But this is so sudden.
BEATRICE. I've waited a week here in Verona for my Tonino to arrive, so that we could go on to Milan together. And I haven't seen the least sign of him. I worry that he might have had second thoughts about running away with me, or that some horrible accident has kept him in Venice. I have no choice but to go back and find out for myself what's happened.
FLORINDO. I'm sorry, but that would be very unwise. What, go back to Venice, when you've just run away from there for Tonino's sake? If your family finds you, you'll be destroyed.
BEATRICE. Venice is a big city; I'll arrive at night, and make sure no one knows I'm there.
FLORINDO. No, Miss Beatrice, I won't let you do it. Tonino sent you to me; he asked me to take care of you and watch over you; if I let you go, I'd be betraying my friend. *(Aside.)* Not to mention my own feelings for her.
BEATRICE. It won't be your fault; I'll find some way to leave you despite all your efforts. I know what time the mail coach leaves, [and the servant I have here in Verona will help me].
FLORINDO. Oh, but it would be the worst thing you could do. Didn't you tell me that on your journey here, this man Lelio was pes-

THE VENETIAN TWINS

tering you all the way? And haven't I seen him myself here in Verona, always hovering around you, to the point where I've had to threaten him once or twice? If you leave on your own, and he finds out, who knows what he might try to do?

BEATRICE. A respectable woman doesn't worry about such things.

FLORINDO. But a woman traveling alone, [with one servant,] no matter how respectable, always looks suspicious, and men are tempted to take advantage.

BEATRICE. I want to go anyway.

FLORINDO. Just wait a few more days.

BEATRICE. Oh, if only I didn't feel in my heart that I've lost my Tonino.

FLORINDO. Pray heaven your heart proves wrong. But if you think you've lost him, why go back to Venice?

BEATRICE. And why stay in Verona?

FLORINDO. Because you may find someone who understands your goodness, and can take the place of your Tonino.

BEATRICE. But that can never be. For me there is only Tonino, or death.

FLORINDO. *(Aside.)* Even so, if she stays and her lover doesn't show up, I can change her mind bit by bit.

BEATRICE. *(Aside.)* I'll get away from him as soon as his back is turned.

FLORINDO. But here comes that silly little fop Lelio. He's always after you. Thank God you have me here!

BEATRICE. Let's leave.

FLORINDO. Oh, no; he'd think we were afraid of him. Stand your ground, and be firm.

BEATRICE. *(Aside.)* Just when I was hoping to escape!

LELIO. *(Entering.)* Beautiful lady of Venice, I have learned from the coachman that you long to go back to your home city. If that's true, please let me help you. I will give you carriages, horses, drivers, servants, money, as much as you want, if you will only grant me the pleasure of accompanying you.

BEATRICE. *(Aside.)* What gall!

FLORINDO. Excuse me, sir. What gives you the right to offer Miss Beatrice these magnificent presents when you see she's with me?

LELIO. What do I care if she's with you? I don't owe you any respect. Who are you: Her brother, a distant relative, a hired escort?

FLORINDO. I'm amazed by your hostile tone. I am a gentleman, signor. I have been ordered to protect this lady.

LELIO. That's a tall order, my friend.

FLORINDO. And just why?

LELIO. Because a man can't protect a lady until he shaves at least once a day.

FLORINDO. Still, I'm ready to deal with you or the rest of your kind.

LELIO. Oh, please, out of my way. *(To BEATRICE.)* Isn't there anything I can get you? Money, clothes, protection? Just ask.

FLORINDO. Don't make me lose my temper.

LELIO. Oh, you're such a polite young man, you couldn't do any such thing. Miss Beatrice, give me your hand, and call me your servant.

BEATRICE. I've never met anyone so rude in my whole life.

LELIO. Love makes people bold. What good are all the rituals of politeness? Come, let's go.

(LELIO tries to take her hand; she draws back.)

FLORINDO. *(Giving him a shove.)* I told you, mind your manners!

LELIO. You told me? You told me, you insect? Anyone who treats me like that pays for it in blood! Do you know who I am? I'm the Marchese Lelio, Signor di Montefresco and Conte di Fontechiara, chief judge of Selva Ombrosa. I have more lands than you have hairs in your tangled-up wig, and gold pieces piled higher than you know how to count.

FLORINDO. And more stupid notions in your head than there are stars in the sky or shells in the sea. *(Aside.)* Thinks I don't know him! Calls himself Conte and Marchese — he's Professor Balanzoni's nephew!

LELIO. Either the lady comes with me, or you're in for trouble.

FLORINDO. I'm here to protect the lady, and anything you have to say will be answered by my sword.

LELIO. Poor baby! I feel sorry for you. So eager to die, at your

THE VENETIAN TWINS 21

tender age.
BEATRICE. *(Softly, to FLORINDO.)* Signor Florindo, don't make him any angrier.
FLORINDO. *(To BEATRICE.)* Don't worry, I'll cut him down to size.
LELIO. You're still young, live a little longer: Leave the lady to me. The world's full of women, but you only get one life.
FLORINDO. My honor's worth more than my life. *(Hand on sword hilt.)* Now leave, or draw your sword.
LELIO. *(Knocking FLORINDO's hand off sword hilt.)* You're beneath me; I wouldn't fight the likes of you.
FLORINDO. Noble or peasant, this is how we treat cowards like you. *(FLORINDO doffs his plumed hat and slaps LELIO with it; LELIO, coughing from plume up nose, responds in kind. In the repeated slaps, somehow the hats get switched. Both stop, realize they are holding each other's hat, smile, exchange hats graciously, and draw swords.)* Now we'll see how brave you are.
LELIO. Holy ancestors, help me put him in his place.

(They raise swords to fight.)

BEATRICE. Oh, how dreadful! There's going to be bloodshed and I don't want to be here. I'll go into that inn over there.

(Unnoticed by combatants, she exits through stage right inn door, [followed by SERVANT]. The two men, each uncertain how to begin, have hardly made more than a few preliminary passes when FLORINDO falls, his slip clearly not due to LELIO's swordsmanship.)

FLORINDO. Ow! I tripped!
LELIO. *(Pointing sword at his chest.)* You're done for, fool!
FLORINDO. I slipped by accident.
LELIO. You were conquered by my skill. Now die —

(TONINO enters, sword in hand, leaping to FLORINDO's defense.)

TONINO. Drop it, drop it! You've got him down, now put up

22 THE VENETIAN TWINS

your sword.
 LELIO. Who asked you to mix in?
 TONINO. I'm a gentleman; my honor wouldn't stand for this offense.
 FLORINDO. What — Tonino — my dear friend —

(FLORINDO gets up.)

TONINO. *(Softly, to FLORINDO.)* Ssh ... yes, it's me, just in time to save your life, but don't say my name out loud. *(Challenging LELIO.)* All right, Signor Frills and Feathers, now it's my turn.
 LELIO. *(Aside.)* He's ruined the whole thing. *(To TONINO.)* But who are you?
 TONINO. *(Hand on heart.)* I'm a man from Venice with a strong heart, and I'm not afraid of you or any of your kind.
 LELIO. I don't want to fight you; I have nothing against you.
 TONINO. But I have something against you, and I want to fight you till you bleed.

(TONINO backs LELIO around the stage in a circle at sword's point.)

LELIO. I think you're crazy. What can you have against me?
 TONINO. You've insulted my friend, and that's the same as insulting me. In Venice, we say "friendship is worth more than life itself," and I wouldn't deserve to be a Venetian if I didn't live by that rule.
 LELIO. But how did I insult this oh so close friend of yours?
 TONINO. You think it's no insult to threaten a man when he's down? To tell him he's done for when he's flat on his back? Up with your sword, let's go.
 FLORINDO. *(To TONINO.)* Dear friend, no, don't put your life in danger for me.
 TONINO. *(Nudging FLORINDO aside.)* Come on, out of the way, fighting this little pepper pot will be as easy as eating a raw egg.
 LELIO. I've stood about as much as I can take of your insolence. You insult my honor and the dignity of my ancestors.
 TONINO. That's right. What'll your mommy say, wittle baby?

THE VENETIAN TWINS

What'll your daddy say, seeing his son a great big coward?
    LELIO. *(Raising sword.)* I swear by heaven —
    TONINO. I swear by six feet under.
    LELIO. Have at you! *(Poises his sword to start.)*
    TONINO. Hooray, let's fight!

(They fight. TONINO disarms LELIO.)

    LELIO. What rotten luck! I'm disarmed.

(He flees into audience, where TONINO pursues him. Possibly an audience member gets drawn into the action when LELIO tries to use him as a shield. Eventually TONINO forces LELIO back up onstage, dismissing the audience member — if he has been dragged up too —with thanks.)

    TONINO. You're disarmed, and that's enough for me. You see how it's done? No anger, no death threats. The honor of beating you is enough for me — and the right to keep your sword as a trophy to remember you by. Just the blade, of course; you can take the scabbard home, or sell it to pay the doctor who treats your nervous breakdown.

(LELIO whines. TONINO laughs and tosses him back his sword.)

    LELIO. *(Snatching it and putting it in scabbard.)* That's enough! I'll have my revenge some other time.
    TONINO. I'll be there. Whenever you call, you'll find me at home.
    LELIO. I'll come, you'll see.

(LELIO starts to leave.)

    TONINO.
"There is no terror, Cassius, in your threats
 For I am arm'd so strong in honesty
 That they pass by me as the idle wind."
    LELIO. *(Aside.)* Quoting Dante! I should have thought of that.

(LELIO exits.)

FLORINDO. My dear friend, you've saved my life!

TONINO. That's all right. Where's Beatrice?

FLORINDO. Beatrice! *(Aside.)* I'd better think fast! *(To TONINO.)* Beatrice who?

TONINO. The young girl I sent you, to take care of for me, the one I helped to escape from her parents in Venice.

FLORINDO. My dear friend — she never arrived.

TONINO. What? Is this some kind of joke?

FLORINDO. It's the truth. I never laid eyes on the lady, and you know how thrilled I would have been to help you out.

TONINO. I know that; it's my mistake. I suppose I'll never find a woman I can trust. I've spent two years courting this one. Her father didn't want me to have her, because he somehow got the idea that I was no good — just because I like to live it up with my friends, and I dabble in this and that. Even so, I'm a gentleman, and I have a sense of honor. So when I saw he would never let me have her, I convinced her to run away. And she packed her bags without a moment's hesitation, and came here. [I had a servant I could trust traveling with her to Verona, while I stayed in Venice so no one would think I was involved.] But a foreign gentleman who also had his eye on the girl got hold of me, suspecting that I had something to do with her escape, and he made a few nasty remarks. One word led to another, until I slapped him so hard I left a bruise. Half of Venice was jabbering about it, and he was ready to nail me any way he could. So I grabbed a gondola and started for Verona without even going home, no money, no clothes, just the little I had with me. I thought I'd find my darling Beatrice here, but it seems she's cheated me too. So now you see, my friend, why you can't call me Tonino for the next two hours; I don't dare let anyone know I'm here.

FLORINDO. And what do you want me to call you?

TONINO. Call me Zanetto.

FLORINDO. Why Zanetto?

TONINO. Because that's the name of my twin brother in Bergamo, who looks just like me. So if they hear you call me Zanetto, they'll think it's him, and I'll be safe from harm.

FLORINDO. Your brother's in Bergamo now?

THE VENETIAN TWINS

TONINO. I think so, but I can't be sure, because we've never really been close. He has more money than I do, but I know my way about the world a little better. Actually, I've heard that he's getting married, but I don't know where or to whom. He's a prize fool, but the lucky woman who snags him will be rolling in it.

FLORINDO. I hope while you're here, my friend, you'll do me the honor of staying at my house.

TONINO. Well, I don't want to put you to any trouble.

FLORINDO. Oh, no, it's a pleasure. Although, to tell you the truth, my father's an old fusspot and hates having visitors.

TONINO. In that case, please don't bother, it's no problem, I'll stay at the inn.

FLORINDO. I'm incredibly sorry, really, if you want —

TONINO. Tonino Bisognosi isn't about to be a burden on his friends. I'm a gentleman: I don't take, I give. Come to Venice, and you'll see what hospitality is. [We open our hearts and our homes to travelers;] we pride ourselves on treating guests so that they'll always speak well of Venice, no matter where they're from. You're my friend; I know you have a good heart. But a good mother doesn't say, "Would you;" she says, "Take."

FLORINDO. But my dear friend, it would be a pleasure: Do come.

TONINO. Let's say that I might. If I can bring myself to do it. I am Tonino, and that's my story. I'd give my life and all my blood for my country first, and then for a friend. Your servant.

(TONINO goes out.)

FLORINDO. *(Alone.)* I feel terribly embarrassed; Tonino was right to reproach me. But I have to be cruel, loving Beatrice as I do. If I brought him home, he'd find out I was betraying him. What would help me is if Tonino leaves and Beatrice stays with me. Then I'd explain the whole thing, and maybe she'd accept me as her lover. I'd better go and find her. I'll make her stay here, in hiding, today and tomorrow. [I'll send her servant away on some errand.] I'd do anything to have this incredible beauty for my own. I'm being irresponsible and betraying my friend, but love's demands are too strong for my heart to resist. I owe Tonino my life, and I'm ready to sacrifice mine for him. Yes, I'm ready to do anything for him — except give up Beatrice. I love her so much!

(FLORINDO goes out. After an instant, ZANETTO comes in silently, sad and lost in thought, stroking the cheek on which he was slapped. LELIO enters, cautiously, and sees him.)

LELIO. *(Mistaking him for TONINO.)* So, you're alone. Now we'll settle our debts.
ZANETTO. Your humble servant, signor.
LELIO. Less talk and more action. Draw your sword.
ZANETTO. Draw? I have no paper.
LELIO. What? Don't be an idiot! Get your hand on the hilt and draw your sword.
ZANETTO. My sword?
LELIO. Yes, your sword.
ZANETTO. But why?
LELIO. Because I won't let anyone call me a coward just because I've lost one round.
ZANETTO. Excuse me, sir, but where are you from?
LELIO. I'm from Rome. Why?
ZANETTO. Because I don't understand one word you're saying.
LELIO. You don't understand me? Maybe you'll understand this!

(LELIO draws his sword, whirls it around flamboyantly.)

ZANETTO. *(Shouts.)* Help! Murder! Quick! He's trying to kill me!
LELIO. What's this! You think it's all a big joke? I'll show you! You may be brave, but right now I could make the god of war surrender, and Jove himself couldn't disarm me. Come on, fight!
ZANETTO. *(Aside.)* First the slap and now the sword! I must look like an easy target.
LELIO. Don't just stand there, come on, fight back.

(LELIO draws ZANETTO's sword and tries to make him take it; ZANETTO recoils.)

THE VENETIAN TWINS

ZANETTO. Euh!
LELIO. Defend yourself, or I'll stab you to death!

(LELIO pokes him lightly with tip of sword before stabbing it into the ground.)

ZANETTO. Ow!

(As LELIO draws his own sword and prepares to thrust, enter FLORINDO, drawing his.)

FLORINDO. If my friend won't fight, I will. Have at you!
LELIO. *(Turning to FLORINDO.)* Your friend's nothing, he's a coward.
ZANETTO. *(To FLORINDO.)* Sir, it's true, he's hit the nail on the head.
FLORINDO. *(To LELIO.)* Liar, insulting a man of such courage.
ZANETTO. *(Aside, referring to FLORINDO.)* Has he ever got me wrong!
LELIO. *(To FLORINDO.)* Then why won't he fight me?
ZANETTO. *(Aside.)* 'Cause I'm afraid.
FLORINDO. Because you aren't worth fighting.
ZANETTO. *(Aside.)* This one's as crazy as the other one.
FLORINDO. *(To LELIO.)* But don't worry, I'll keep your sword busy.
LELIO. I'm ready for you, or a hundred like you!

(They fight. This time the sword fight itself spills into the aisles. ZANETTO comes downstage, cheering like a fan at a tennis match.)

ZANETTO. Bravo, terrific, move, do it, cut him to pieces.

(The DUELERS clamber back onstage, where this time LELIO trips, in the same spot where FLORINDO fell earlier.)

FLORINDO. *(As LELIO falls.)* Behold how the mighty are fallen.
LELIO. Today fate is unkind to the brave.
FLORINDO. Your life is in my hands.

ZANETTO. *(Who has moved upstage when the DUELERS came back on.)* Go on, get 'im! Punch a hole in his breadbasket!

FLORINDO. *(Shocked.)* A gentleman doesn't do things like that.

ZANETTO. That gentleman down there wanted to carve me to bits.

FLORINDO. But when you brought him down because he was threatening my life, you didn't do the same to him.

ZANETTO. You're crazy. Go on, get 'im.

FLORINDO. No. *(To LELIO, helping him up and giving him back his sword.)* Live. And remember that you owe me your life.

LELIO. You're a man worth fighting. But your friend's still a lily-livered, chicken-hearted coward.

(LELIO goes out.)

ZANETTO. *(Calling after him.)* Anything you say.

FLORINDO. But my dear friend, what's gotten into you? Is it a disguise? Or was it just some mad impulse?

ZANETTO. Signor, I wasn't pretending. I've never been so frightened in my life. If you hadn't come, he'd have me pushin' up daisies right now.

FLORINDO. I'm glad I saved your life.

ZANETTO. And bless you for it. Let me kiss the hand that rescued me.

FLORINDO. I only did for you what you did for me; fair's fair. You saved my life, I saved yours.

ZANETTO. I saved your life?

FLORINDO. That first time, when you rescued me from Lelio.

ZANETTO. Somehow I don't recall.

FLORINDO. You modest types always forget the good you do. *(FLORINDO gets ZANETTO's sword and hands it back to him; helps him fit it in scabbard.)* But I would advise you to leave Verona, friend, because someone might have recognized you.

[ZANETTO. That fellow apparently thought he recognized me.

FLORINDO. But if they recognize you, watch out.]

ZANETTO. This gets worse and worse.

FLORINDO. It's no little thing to give someone a slap in the face.

ZANETTO. *(Stroking his cheek.)* It's no little thing to get one.

THE VENETIAN TWINS

FLORINDO. What, someone's slapped you?

ZANETTO. Oh, sir, yes. You didn't think … that *I'd* slap someone, did you?

FLORINDO. That's what I thought.

ZANETTO. Oh no, no no, they got me.

FLORINDO. And you haven't seen the lady again?

ZANETTO. Oh, no sir, I have *not* seen her again.

FLORINDO. *(Aside.)* Where can Beatrice be? I couldn't find her either.

ZANETTO. And I don't care if I never see her again.

FLORINDO. Yes, that's good thinking. Get her out of your mind. Take my advice, go back home.

ZANETTO. Just what I said to myself.

FLORINDO. And if there's any way I can help you —

ZANETTO. Thanks, but no.

FLORINDO. Well, goodbye then.

ZANETTO. My most humble gratitude.

FLORINDO. *(Aside, as he goes out.)* He seems to have lost his mind. Oh, love plays nasty tricks on us.

ZANETTO. *(Alone.)* If that gentleman hadn't shown up, I'd be history. I think everybody in town must know by now that the young lady slapped me. Oh, well. At least this young man's on my side. He tells me I should get out. But I think I like Rosaura, slap or no slap, and I think I'd be awful happy if she was my wife. What really annoys me is that Arlecchino hasn't shown up yet with my money and my clothes. Then I could make her happy by giving her a little present.

PANCRAZIO. *(Entering; aside.)* There's that nitwit Zanetto. Still hanging around this house, can't tear himself away.

ZANETTO. She slapped me, so she must not like me. But wait, my mother used to slap me a lot, and she loved me. [And after all, her slaps didn't kill me.] Oh, I really am crazy. I didn't mean to offend her. I'll go right now and apologize to her.

(ZANETTO turns toward PROFESSOR's house.)

PANCRAZIO. Where are you going, young man?

ZANETTO. Going to see my sweetie.

30 THE VENETIAN TWINS

PANCRAZIO. The one who slapped you?
ZANETTO. Yes, that's her.
PANCRAZIO. And you've decided to make up with her, and marry her?
ZANETTO. You guessed it.
PANCRAZIO. You like the young lady?
ZANETTO. Pretty much.
PANCRAZIO. You long for her?
ZANETTO. And how!
PANCRAZIO. You'll gladly marry her?
ZANETTO. You bet!
PANCRAZIO. You poor thing, I feel so sorry for you.
ZANETTO. Beg pardon?
PANCRAZIO. You're on the edge of the abyss.
ZANETTO. What's that?
PANCRAZIO. You don't want to get married?
ZANETTO. Sure do.
PANCRAZIO. Then you're ruined, you poor unhappy creature.
ZANETTO. But why?
PANCRAZIO. *(Leading ZANETTO away from PROFESSOR's door.)* I live only to help others; let me warn you, as a friend and a brother: [You're about to commit an act of enormous insanity.
ZANETTO. But how?
PANCRAZIO. Do you know what it is to be married?
ZANETTO. To be married … sure I do … it's, well, how do I put it … it's just … having a wife.
PANCRAZIO. Oh, if you really knew what marriage is, knew what a wife is, you wouldn't talk about it so calmly.
ZANETTO. But … what are you saying?]
PANCRAZIO. Marriage is a chain that locks a man up like a slave in the galleys.
ZANETTO. Marriage is?
PANCRAZIO. Marriage is.
ZANETTO. You're kidding!
PANCRAZIO. Marriage is a lead weight that makes you sweat all day and stay awake all night. It weighs on your spirit, it weighs on your body, it weighs on your mind and it weighs on your wallet.
ZANETTO. Suffering shellfish!

THE VENETIAN TWINS

PANCRAZIO. And the girl who seems so pretty and gentle to you, you wouldn't believe what she's really like.

ZANETTO. Oh, dear sir, do tell me.

PANCRAZIO. The girl is a witch, a Circe who loves only herself, and lures men on only to cheat them.

ZANETTO. That girl?

PANCRAZIO. That girl.

ZANETTO. You don't say!

PANCRAZIO. Those two sparkling eyes of hers are two fiery flames that scorch you bit by bit until you're all burned up.

ZANETTO. Her eyes — two fiery flames ...

PANCRAZIO. Her mouth is like a vial of poison that pours itself slowly in your ear, then works its way down to your heart until it kills you.

ZANETTO. Her mouth — a vial of poison ...

PANCRAZIO. Her cheeks, so lovely and rosy, are witch's spells that hypnotize you.

ZANETTO. Her cheeks — witch's spells — hypnotize ...

PANCRAZIO. Whenever a woman comes toward you, always keep in mind that she's a mad fury, coming to tear you to shreds.

ZANETTO. The evil slut!

PANCRAZIO. And when a woman moves to embrace you, she's a demon that wants to drag you down to hell.

ZANETTO. Keep her away!

PANCRAZIO. Think it over, and think it over carefully.

ZANETTO. I've already thought.

PANCRAZIO. No more women.

ZANETTO. No more women.

PANCRAZIO. No more marriage.

ZANETTO. No more marriage.

PANCRAZIO. Years from now, you'll thank me for this.

ZANETTO. God sent you to me.

PANCRAZIO. Be wise; go now. And may heaven bless you.

ZANETTO. You're like my father; I owe you so much.

PANCRAZIO. Here's my hand; kiss it.

ZANETTO. *(Covering his hand with kisses.)* Oh, dear friend! God bless you!

PANCRAZIO. Women — ?

ZANETTO. *(Shuddering.)* Ugh!
PANCRAZIO. Marriage — ?
ZANETTO. *(Shrinking in horror.)* Ooh!
PANCRAZIO. No more — ?
ZANETTO. No more.
PANCRAZIO. Promise?
ZANETTO. I swear.
PANCRAZIO. Bravo, bravo, bravo!

(PANCRAZIO goes out.)

ZANETTO. *(Alone.)* Holy jumping mackerel! If that good man hadn't come my way, I would have gotten myself into a fine mess. Marriage ... it weighs on you here, it weighs on you there, it weighs on your mind, it weighs on your wallet ... women ... witches, furies, demons. Ooh, what a hell of a mess!

BEATRICE. *(Coming in and seeing ZANETTO, whom she mistakes for TONINO.)* Oh, I'm so happy! My darling, my husband. When did you get here?

ZANETTO. Away, keep off.

BEATRICE. What? Don't you love me anymore? Didn't you come here just so we could get married?

ZANETTO. Right, chained, like the galley slaves. Too late; I've found out what it means.

BEATRICE. Chains? Who said anything about chains? What about all your promises?

ZANETTO. Promises? What promises?

BEATRICE. Of marriage.

ZANETTO. Right, marriage. A weight on your mind and a weight on your wallet.

BEATRICE. Stop this, look at me. Don't make fun of me or you'll strike me dead.

ZANETTO. *(Aside, covering his eyes.)* She probably wants to burn me with the flames in her eyes.

BEATRICE. Don't you trust me? What can I say to make you believe me?

ZANETTO. Close your mouth, that poison pot, I don't want your spells to get my heart drunk.

THE VENETIAN TWINS

BEATRICE. Oh, God! What are you saying? Doesn't it hurt you to make me flush with shame this way?

ZANETTO. Stand back! *(Aside.)* If she goes all red, I'll know she's a witch.

BEATRICE. *(Reaching toward ZANETTO.)* I'm desperate. For pity's sake, hear me out.

ZANETTO. Away, you demon! You want to drag me down to hell!

(ZANETTO runs off.)

BEATRICE. *(Alone.)* Can I hear all this and not die? What am I to think of my Tonino? Either he's gone mad, or someone has told him evil rumors about me. [I'm so miserable, what can I do?] I'll follow him from a distance and try to find out the truth any way I can. Love, it was my bad luck that you made me run away from my home, my family, and my friends; now I beg you, help me in this terrible danger, take my blood as your reward, drain it away, but don't let me live to hear such insults from my beloved Tonino!

(BEATRICE dashes out after him.)

CURTAIN

ACT II

Scene 1

(A[nother] street. The PROFESSOR's house at one side, an inn with its sign out at the other.
ARLECCHINO enters, dressed for travel, with a PORTER carrying a trunk and a short cloak.)

ARLECCHINO. At last I'm here in Verona. What a beautiful city! Where else could Cupid shoot an arrow that strikes a man's heart before he's even seen the bow? Where else can I love a woman I've never seen, and be about to marry one I've never met?

PORTER. Let's get a move on; I've got other jobs to do, and I have to earn my bread.

ARLECCHINO. But I don't know where that nitwit I work for is staying. Listen, friend, do you know a Signor Zanetto Bisognosi?

PORTER. Never heard of him. Wouldn't know where to look.

ARLECCHINO. Well, that's my boss. He just got here from Bergamo to get married; he gets the lady of the house, and I get her maid, just to keep it all in the family. But he arrived ahead of me, so here I am with all his stuff, and I don't know where he's staying, or how to find him.

PORTER. If you don't know, I don't know. Verona's a big city; you'll get awful tired trying to find him.

ARLECCHINO. Talk about luck! There he is now. Move over this way; I want to play a trick on him; let's see if he recognizes me.

PORTER. Isn't it risky playing tricks on your master?

ARLECCHINO. Oh, he's more like a friend. Come on, watch, we'll have a little fun.

PORTER. Well, hurry it up, I haven't got any time to lose.

ARLECCHINO. Oh, relax, you got your money.

(They move into an upstage corner; TONINO enters.)

TONINO. It's incredible! I can't find Beatrice anywhere. Can she have been cheating me all along, was it all a trick? *(ARLECCHINO, concealing his face in his cloak, walks toward TONINO, in an exaggeratedly disguised manner.)* What's this one up to? Does he want something from me? *(ARLECCHINO turns and passes TONINO again, this time with a rough, menacing air.)* Could that fellow I slapped have sent a killer to Verona to hunt me down? *(ARLECCHINO walks by a third time, stamping his foot.)* What is it, sir? What do you want?

ARLECCHINO. *(Aside, laughing.)* Oh, what an idiot, he doesn't know me.

TONINO. Come on, talk, what do you want with me? *(ARLECCHINO makes some grand gesture. TONINO draws his sword.)* Let's see how brave you really are.

ARLECCHINO. Easy, easy; put that away. *(Throwing off cloak and tossing it to PORTER.)* Don't you know me?

TONINO. Who are you? I don't know you.

ARLECCHINO. What! You don't know me?

TONINO. No sir; I never saw you before in my life.

ARLECCHINO. *(Aside.)* The air in this city must have turned his brain.

TONINO. Do you mind telling me who you are? And what you want?

ARLECCHINO. *(Laughing.)* Tell me, have you been drinking?

TONINO. Don't get fresh with me, unless you like walking on your knees.

ARLECCHINO. So you really don't know me?

TONINO. I already told you, I don't know you.

ARLECCHINO. Well, you will know me. *(Gleefully offers him a small casket of jewels.)* Here's your stuff: Now do you know me?

TONINO. *(Aside, looking in.)* What fabulous jewels! Can he be a peddler?

ARLECCHINO. Well? Do you know me yet?

TONINO. No, sir; I still don't know you.

THE VENETIAN TWINS

ARLECCHINO. No? Well, you will. *(Hands him a purse full of money.)* Here's your money. Now do you know me?

TONINO. *(Aside, hefting it.)* A lot of money in here! *(To ARLECCHINO.)* No sir, I still don't know you.

ARLECCHINO. Damn it all to hell! You do know me! *That's* your trunk, and you know me!

TONINO. Give me all the trunks you want and I still don't know you.

ARLECCHINO. Are you crazy, or just drunk?

TONINO. You're the one who's drunk or crazy. Your jewels and your money don't belong to me. I'm a gentleman and I don't want your things. Take them back, and give them to whoever owns them.

ARLECCHINO. But you're the one who owns them; this is all your stuff. The jewels, the money, the trunk — it's everything you gave me to bring here, and I did what I was told. So tell me, where are you staying?

TONINO. At that inn.

ARLECCHINO. So should I have him bring the trunk there?

TONINO. Take it anywhere you want.

ARLECCHINO. But you don't know me?

TONINO. No, I don't know you.

ARLECCHINO. Huh! Goddam halfwit. I'm going to the inn. I'll put the trunk in your room, I'll take a nap, and when you've sobered up, you'll know me.

(ARLECCHINO goes into the inn, taking the trunk and cloak.)

TONINO. Well, this is a nice mess. A casket of jewels, a purse full of money, it would have made a good haul for somebody, but I'm a gentleman, and I don't take other people's things. That fellow must be crazy. God knows how he got his hands on that money and those jewels. If I don't take care of them, he'll probably hand them over to some crook or other. But I'll take care of them, and try to find out whom they really belong to[, so he can get them back as soon as possible].

COLOMBINA. *(Entering.)* Signor Zanetto, your servant.

TONINO. You mean me?

COLOMBINA. Yes sir, you. You are Signor Zanetto Bisognosi,

aren't you?
 TONINO. Yes, of course, at your service. *(Aside.)* She's mistaken me for my brother, that's not bad.
 COLOMBINA. If you're willing, my mistress would like to speak to you.
 TONINO. *(Aside.)* I see. The sort of thing that happens when a man's away from home. *(To COLOMBINA.)* With pleasure. As I have no other appointments, I'm at your service.
 COLOMBINA. What beautiful jewels you have there, Signor Zanetto.
 TONINO. *(Aside.)* Oh, now I understand. She saw the jewels from her balcony and sent the maid to try and snag them.
 COLOMBINA. Of course, I'm sure you brought them to present to Miss Rosaura.
 TONINO. Is that your mistress?
 COLOMBINA. My mistress? Of course.
 TONINO. *(Aside.)* She thinks they're my jewels; she's picked the wrong pigeon this time. But this could be fun. *(To COLOMBINA.)* They might be for her, if it feels right to me.
 COLOMBINA. In that case, it's guaranteed, she's such a lovely young thing.
 TONINO. *(Aside.)* Bravo! She certainly knows how to peddle the merchandise. *(To COLOMBINA, who is trying to lead him into the house.)* But tell me, how do I settle the account?
 COLOMBINA. What account?
 TONINO. The money.
 COLOMBINA. Miss Rosaura doesn't need any money.
 TONINO. *(Aside.)* Ah, it's the jewels she's after. *(To COLOMBINA.)* So your mistress must be very rich.
 COLOMBINA. Well, of course, her father's a professor.
 TONINO. Her father's a professor?
 COLOMBINA. *(Again trying to lead TONINO into the house.)* Oh, didn't you know that?
 TONINO. But wouldn't the professor get all upset if he sees me in the house?
 COLOMBINA. Why, that's just what he wants. He actually also sent me out here, to invite you to dine with him.
 TONINO. *(Aside.)* Bravi! They're all in it together, the father, the

THE VENETIAN TWINS

daughter, and the maid. I'd sooner walk into a lion's cage. *(To CO-LOMBINA.)* Listen, my girl, tell your mistress I'll come some other time.

COLOMBINA. Oh, no sir, no, she wants you to come right now. [And you're a good man, you'll win her eventually.

TONINO. All right, just let me put these jewels away safely and I'll be right with you.

COLOMBINA. Oh, but they're so beautiful! You should really bring a few with you, if you want to make her happy.

TONINO. *(Aside, closing the casket.)* That's it, I knew it. They're after the jewels. But I'm not taking any risks. They're not mine; I'll play this discreetly. I know how the world works.]

(The PROFESSOR enters from his house.)

COLOMBINA. Oh, Professor, Signor Zanetto's here, but he won't come into the house, though I've talked myself hoarse inviting him.

PROFESSOR. Oh, do come in, Signor Zanetto, my daughter's expecting you.

TONINO. *(Aside.)* Bravo, bravo, they're all so good at it.

PROFESSOR. The way you hesitate is a terrible insult to the dear girl.

TONINO. *(Aside.)* Better and better!

PROFESSOR. Do you want her to come out and court you on the street?

TONINO. Oh, no! I suppose I'd better go in.

PROFESSOR. Wonderful! Walk this way.

TONINO. It's all right with you?

PROFESSOR. Night-time, daytime, anytime.

TONINO. Always open house, eh?

PROFESSOR. For Signor Zanetto the door is never locked.

TONINO. But only for me?

PROFESSOR. Of course, only for you.

TONINO. And not for anyone else?

PROFESSOR. Except for a few close friends, of course.

TONINO. I see; I thought there was a catch to it. All right.

PROFESSOR. Well, come along.

TONINO. And I can leave and come back?
PROFESSOR. Whenever you like.
TONINO. And I can take off my coat and relax?
PROFESSOR. Of course.
TONINO. And get a bite to eat?
PROFESSOR. My dear sir!
TONINO. Very good. I'm at your service.

(TONINO starts to go into the house.)

PROFESSOR. If you don't mind, Signor Zanetto, just one more thing.
TONINO. *(Aside.)* Now comes the touch. He wants his share in advance. *(To PROFESSOR.)* Yes?
PROFESSOR. Pardon me for asking, but — do you have some pretty little gift in that casket?
TONINO. *(Aside.)* Aha, they tipped him off about the jewels. *(To PROFESSOR.)* A few odds and ends. Some baubles.
PROFESSOR. Good, good. My daughter will be so pleased.
TONINO. *(Aside.)* He must not be a Professor of morals. *(To PROFESSOR.)* Don't worry, if she's reasonable, she'll have them. *(Aside.)* When Hell freezes over.
PROFESSOR. After all, with ladies we must be generous.
TONINO. I'm a gentleman, my friend. Neither you nor your daughter will have anything to complain about.
PROFESSOR. I'm sure of it.
COLOMBINA. That's enough talk. Go on in.
TONINO. What, by myself?
PROFESSOR. Feel free.
TONINO. Thank you, that's very kind. *(Aside.)* Such nice manners they have here. They smile and take the jewels, and I probably get dumped in the river in a sack.

(TONINO goes into the PROFESSOR's house.)

COLOMBINA. It seems to me that this Signor Zanetto doesn't love Miss Rosaura very much.
PROFESSOR. Why not?

THE VENETIAN TWINS

COLOMBINA. Didn't you see what we had to go through to get him in the house? Go on in sir, yes sir, your servant sir. It makes me sick to my stomach.

PROFESSOR. On the other hand, I can see why. Do you know what Rosaura did to him?

COLOMBINA. No, what?

PROFESSOR. She gave him a terrific slap in the face.

COLOMBINA. But why?

PROFESSOR. I think he was trying to hold her hand.

COLOMBINA. In that case Miss Rosaura was right. And furthermore, if you'll pardon me for saying so, you shouldn't have sent him in to be alone with her.

PROFESSOR. But they won't be alone. Signor Pancrazio's there to keep an eye on them.

COLOMBINA. To hell with your Signor Pancrazio.

PROFESSOR. Why do you talk that way? What did he ever do to you?

COLOMBINA. I just hate the sight of him. Pompous old hypocrite ... and besides —

PROFESSOR. And besides what?

COLOMBINA. He's said things to me —

PROFESSOR. What kind of things? Tell me.

COLOMBINA. And he likes to put his hands everywhere.

PROFESSOR. Bite your sinful tongue! You shouldn't talk that way about a gentleman who's the picture of honesty and decency. You should respect him and obey him just as you do me. He's a good man, and you are a foolish chatterbox.

(He goes into the house.)

COLOMBINA. Whatever my master may think, I'm still convinced that Signor Pancrazio is a fake and up to no good.

ARLECCHINO. *(Coming in.)* Where the hell can that madman have gone? I've been waiting an hour, and there's still no sign of him.

COLOMBINA. *(Aside, seeing him.)* Hmm, short, dark and handsome.

ARLECCHINO. Let me ask this girl if she's seen him. *(To COLOMBINA.)* Excuse me, sweetheart, but do you know a Signor

Zanetto Bisognosi?
>COLOMBINA. Of course I know him.
>ARLECCHINO. You do? Have you seen him lately?
>COLOMBINA. I have.
>ARLECCHINO. And would you happen to know where I might find him?
>COLOMBINA. He's in that house right there.
>ARLECCHINO. Whose house is that?
>COLOMBINA. Miss Rosaura's house, his fiancée.
>ARLECCHINO. And do you know her, Miss Rosaura?
>COLOMBINA. I know her very well.
>ARLECCHINO. And do you happen to know her maid?
>COLOMBINA. Haven't you guessed? I am her maid.
>ARLECCHINO. What? You — you're Miss — Colombina?
>COLOMBINA. That's me, Colombina.
>ARLECCHINO. And do you know who I am?
>COLOMBINA. I give up, who?
>ARLECCHINO. Arlecchino Bartocchio.
>COLOMBINA. You're Arlecchino?
>ARLECCHINO. That's me.
>COLOMBINA. My groom!
>ARLECCHINO. My bride!
>COLOMBINA. Oh, darling!
>ARLECCHINO. Oh, dearest!
>COLOMBINA. Oh, what a treat!
>ARLECCHINO. Oh, what a relief!
>COLOMBINA. When did you get here?
>ARLECCHINO. First things first, let's go in the house, then we can talk.
>COLOMBINA. Wait a second. I'll just run and tell my mistress you're here. Then I can bring you in.
>ARLECCHINO. I should talk to my master too.
>COLOMBINA. Don't move, I'll be right back.
>ARLECCHINO. You're so pretty! I'm really glad.
>COLOMBINA. Oh, go on, don't tease me.
>ARLECCHINO. I'll marry you with pleasure.
>COLOMBINA. You really like me?
>ARLECCHINO. Yes, yes, don't make me suffer, go.

THE VENETIAN TWINS

COLOMBINA. I'm going, I'm going. *(Aside.)* He's really adorable.

(COLOMBINA goes into the house.)

ARLECCHINO. Good luck, you've come to me at last. She is beautiful. And how! She's as rapeable as Lucrece. After all, Lucrece only appealed to Sixtus, but this girl could appeal to at least seven of us.
COLOMBINA. *(Calling from house.)* Arlecchino, come in, come in. My mistress says it's all right.
ARLECCHINO. Coming, dear, coming.

(He is about to go into the house when ZANETTO suddenly appears at the other side of the stage and recognizes him from the back.)

ZANETTO. Hey! Arlecchino!
ARLECCHINO. *(Turning around.)* Sir?
ZANETTO. When?
ARLECCHINO. What?
ZANETTO. You're here.
ARLECCHINO. You're there?
ZANETTO. Of course.
ARLECCHINO. Not in the house?
ZANETTO. Where?
ARLECCHINO. In there.
ZANETTO. Oh, no!
ARLECCHINO. *(Aside.)* Getting back at me for my joke!
ZANETTO. Where's my things?
ARLECCHINO. Where else? At the inn.
ZANETTO. Where?
ARLECCHINO. What a dimwit! There, at the Two-Headed Calf.
ZANETTO. Everything?
ARLECCHINO. Everything.
ZANETTO. With the money and the jewels?
ARLECCHINO. *(Aside.)* The idiot's losing his memory! *(To ZANETTO.)* With the money and the jewels.
ZANETTO. Let's go see.

ARLECCHINO. Fine, let's go.
ZANETTO. You have the key?
ARLECCHINO. To what?
ZANETTO. To my room.
ARLECCHINO. Me? No.
ZANETTO. And you just left the money and the jewels there?
ARLECCHINO. Well, where else should I leave them?
ZANETTO. Where else??
ARLECCHINO. Oh, fine.
ZANETTO. Oh, great.
ARLECCHINO. But don't *you* have the money and the jewels?
ZANETTO. Why? You never gave them to me!
ARLECCHINO. *(Aside.)* If he's not crazy I am!
ZANETTO. Well, where are the jewels, damn it! You did bring them?
ARLECCHINO. Of course I brought them.
ZANETTO. Then where are they?
ARLECCHINO. Look, sir, let's go in there before I lose my temper.
ZANETTO. Well, there's no need to get huffy all of a sudden. They must be in my room.
ARLECCHINO. Yes, they must be in your room.
ZANETTO. *(Going into the inn.)* Well, I'll go see. What a halfwit!
ARLECCHINO. Go and see, Mr. Genius!

(ARLECCHINO follows him into inn.)

COLOMBINA. *(At house door.)* Arlecchino, where are you? Well, that's nice! He's gone. A fine lover they picked out for me. But where can he have gone? Oh, well, never mind, he'll turn up; and if he doesn't turn up, well — *(Looking over audience.)* — a girl like me doesn't have to look far to find a husband.

(COLOMBINA goes back into the house.)

THE VENETIAN TWINS

Scene 2

(A room in the PROFESSOR's house.)

TONINO. *(Seated alone, waiting.)* She hasn't shown up yet, and I've been waiting here for an hour. I don't know if they think that I'm a total idiot, or that I'll pay more if the goods are hard to get. Well, they can't fool Tonino. I'm from Venice and I'm a gentleman, and that's my story. Let's see some action. Anyone home in there?

BRIGHELLA. *(Entering slowly.)* At your service, sir. What would you like?

TONINO. And who're you?

BRIGHELLA. I'm the butler here.

TONINO. *(Aside.)* And I'm Marie Antoinette. They've even got him in livery! *(Lazzo: During aside, BRIGHELLA stares intensely at TONINO, trying to determine whether or not he's ZANETTO; turning back to him after saying the line, TONINO catches him at it and BRIGHELLA quickly turns away and pretends to be doing something else. To BRIGHELLA.)* Tell me, friend, is your mistress going to show her pretty face, or should I just leave?

BRIGHELLA. *(Beginning to move, slowly.)* I'll go get her right away, sir. *(Stopping and leaning over TONINO as if for an intimate chat.)* You see, I've been working here for years, but I used to be servant to the Bisognosi family.

TONINO. Do you know me?

BRIGHELLA. I used to know your brother, sir. A really genteel young fellow.

TONINO. Where did you know him?

BRIGHELLA. In Venice.

TONINO. You mean you knew him as a boy?

BRIGHELLA. Even when he was all grown up ... but here comes my mistress.

TONINO. Wait, wait, talk to me. You knew him in Venice when he was all grown up?

BRIGHELLA. Sorry, I've got to go. We can talk later. Your servant.

(BRIGHELLA goes out, moving more rapidly than expected.)

46   **THE VENETIAN TWINS**

TONINO. What the hell was he talking about? Either he's crazy, or there's something fishy going on around here.

ROSAURA. *(Coming in.)* Signor Zanetto, I'm so sorry to keep you waiting.

TONINO. Oh, it's all right, Miss, I'm used to it. *(Aside.)* What a beauty! Everything in the right place!

ROSAURA. *(Aside.)* What a strange look on his face. He must still be angry about the slap.

TONINO. *(Aside.)* I'm staying in Verona. I can't leave this!

ROSAURA. I hope I haven't inconvenienced you.

TONINO. Not at all, Miss, not at all. In fact, I consider myself lucky to be allowed the pleasure of your company.

ROSAURA. *(Aside.)* What an odd compliment! Can he be making fun of me? I'd better play along, just to humor him.

TONINO. *(Aside.)* From her look you'd think she was modesty itself.

ROSAURA. It was actually my father who made me invite you into the house.

TONINO. You mean you wouldn't have asked me if he hadn't insisted?

ROSAURA. I certainly would never have been that forward.

TONINO. *(Aside.)* The road to hell is paved with friendly fathers. *(To ROSAURA.)* So you don't feel drawn to me at all yourself?

ROSAURA. Oh, no, I have great respect for you.

TONINO. All the better. *(Leaning toward her.)* And can I hope for some sign of that respect?

ROSAURA. You can hope for everything, if my father approves.

TONINO. *(Aside.)* [The poor thing! I hate to see her suffer.] The father calls the shots and she pays the price. *(To ROSAURA.)* I'm sorry, but I don't think I made myself clear. Exactly how are we supposed to behave?

ROSAURA. In terms of what?

TONINO. In terms of our ... relationship.

ROSAURA. That you have to discuss with my father.

TONINO. I see, he's the one who makes the arrangements. He does it all.

ROSAURA. Of course he does.

TONINO. [*(Aside.)* Oh, that conniving Professor!] *(To ROSAURA.)*

THE VENETIAN TWINS

But what if he walks in on us while we're —

ROSAURA. While we're what?

TONINO. While we're having a little fun.

ROSAURA. Be careful. Remember that slap.

TONINO. *(Aside.)* What! Even she knows I slapped that man in Venice. It must be in the newspaper. *(To ROSAURA.)* Oh, I never remember little things like that.

ROSAURA. Well, I remember it perfectly.

TONINO. [But why does it matter?

ROSAURA. It matters because you lost your self-control.]

TONINO. But my dear girl, such things can't happen when I'm with you.

ROSAURA. Really? Even so, it's best to be cautious.

TONINO. [I don't know what to say.] You're right. I won't do it again. As long as you say you love me.

ROSAURA. [Well, I wouldn't be too sure of that.

TONINO. *(Sighs.)* Oh, dear ...

ROSAURA. Why so sad?

TONINO. Because I'm afraid you say the same thing to all the men.

ROSAURA. All what men? Really, you amaze me.

TONINO. Gently, gently. Show a little sympathy.

ROSAURA. What could possibly have made you say such a thing?

TONINO. Oh, come, I just got to Verona yesterday; you'll never convince me that you fell in love with me at first sight.]

ROSAURA. In fact, the minute I saw you, I felt something clutch at my heart.

TONINO. *(Aside.)* Should I believe her or not? Oh, women, women, can you ever trust them?

ROSAURA. And what about you, Signor Zanetto, do you love me?

TONINO. You're so beautiful, so gentle and graceful, a man who didn't love you would be a lump of stucco.

ROSAURA. And what will you give me to prove your love?

TONINO. *(Aside.)* I don't know if she wants kisses or cash. *(To ROSAURA.)* Anything; just ask me.

ROSAURA. It's up to you to show your affection.

TONINO. *(Aside.)* I understand. Let's see how she reacts to this.

(To ROSAURA, opening casket.) If it isn't too forward of me, I have a few jewels here that I'd like to offer you.

ROSAURA. Beautiful, really beautiful. And did you mean them as a gift for me?

TONINO. Just ask, and they're yours.

ROSAURA. I am delighted to accept such a precious gift, and I'll treasure them always as the first token of your love.

TONINO. That's fine; we can look at them later. *(Aside.)* She didn't need to be begged to take them, the sweet, modest little thing!

ROSAURA. But tell me, don't you have some other sign of your devotion to offer me?

TONINO. *(Aside.)* She wants to clean me out on the first try. *(To ROSAURA.)* Oh, yes, I have a sum of money, if you want it, that's yours too.

ROSAURA. Oh, no, no, that you must give to my father. I don't deal with money.

TONINO. *(Aside.)* That's nice, she runs the business and the father keeps the cash box. [*(To ROSAURA.)* I'll do as you request.]

ROSAURA. But you don't seem to want to give me what I ask.

TONINO. Oh, hell! Do you want the shirt off my back? It's yours.

ROSAURA. Oh, no, I don't want your shirt, or even your jacket. I want you.

TONINO. Me? I'm all yours.

ROSAURA. Then we can settle things today.

TONINO. Right now, if you want.

ROSAURA. I'm ready.

TONINO. And I'm as ready as I'll ever be.

ROSAURA. Will you give me your hand?

TONINO. The hand, the feet, and everything else you could ask for.

ROSAURA. Then we must call the witnesses.

TONINO. Whoa. What do we need witnesses for?

ROSAURA. Because they have to be there.

TONINO. Where?

ROSAURA. At our wedding.

TONINO. Wedding? Back up a little.

ROSAURA. But didn't you just say you were ready?

THE VENETIAN TWINS

TONINO. I'm ready, yes; but marriage, all of a sudden —

ROSAURA. Get out, get out, I can see it's all a joke to you.

TONINO. *(Aside.)* I don't dislike her at all, and maybe in time I'd go so far as to tie the knot. But what I definitely don't like is the casual way they invite men into this house.

ROSAURA. You change your mind so fast, Signor Zanetto.

TONINO. Change my mind? No, really, I'm faithful and loyal. I always honor my commitments. But, as you probably know much better than I, these things call for a little give and take. [You have to think about them, I mean,] let's not be too hasty with something so important.

ROSAURA. And then you say you haven't changed your mind. First you're ready right now, you don't want any ceremony or contract, and a minute later you're asking for give and take, and saying we have to think about it.

TONINO. Well, if you say I have to decide right now, then I would say: That's that. I mean, please don't be angry, but —

ROSAURA. No no, say what you mean.

TONINO. If you would be willing to —

ROSAURA. Not a chance of it, until we're married.

TONINO. Not at all?

ROSAURA. Absolutely not.

TONINO. Well, but the jewels?

ROSAURA. If that's what you had in mind when you gave them to me, take them back, I don't want them.

TONINO. To say that is so honorable it makes you deserve them even more. You're a thoroughly fine young woman, and it's a pity your father's such an old scoundrel.

ROSAURA. What did my father ever do to make you say that?

TONINO. You think it's nothing? Shamelessly hauling a strange man into the house and shoving a young girl into his arms?

ROSAURA. But he did that because we're engaged.

TONINO. [You amaze me;] that's not true at all. We never discussed anything of the kind.

ROSAURA. But didn't you arrange it all in your letters?

TONINO. Miss, no, it's just not true. [Maybe he dreamed it, or meant to do it. But I think he's up to no good:] He saw I had a little money, thought he could get it away from me, and so he tries to use your incredible beauty to turn a dishonest penny.

ROSAURA. Signor Zanetto, what you're saying is terrible.

TONINO. What I'm saying is only too true. But I can see that you deserve better, with your beauty and your honesty; you wouldn't stoop to such tricks. So be strong, if you really love me; in time you may yet become my wife.

ROSAURA. I'm so [upset and] embarrassed. If I hadn't assumed you were my fiancé, do you think I'd ever have been brave enough to look you in the eye? If my father's deceived me, God forgive him, but if this is some trick of yours, it's beyond cruelty. So think about what you're saying, and always remember that I love you, with a love as honest and virtuous as any in the world.

(ROSAURA dashes out.)

TONINO. *(Alone.)* Did you ever see such a modest daughter with such a scoundrel for a father? Marry her? Tonino, pull yourself together. When you do it, it's done. But I've got to think it out. There's Beatrice, who ran away from her family because I promised my love to her. But where is she? Where's she gone? Did she really run away for me, or was it for somebody else altogether? [She never got here; I have no idea where she is. Maybe she betrayed me; that wouldn't be a surprise.] She could have been stringing me along; that's how women are, and that's that.

BRIGHELLA. *(Entering.)* Can I get you anything, signor?

TONINO. No, my friend. I'm just leaving.

BRIGHELLA. So soon?

TONINO. What else can I do?

BRIGHELLA. You won't stay and dine with the Professor?

TONINO. No, thank you very much. You can tell the Professor he's not the sort of person I care to dine with.

BRIGHELLA. What do you mean?

TONINO. You know exactly what I mean.

BRIGHELLA. I'm astounded. I don't know what you're saying. He just told me to make sure you have everything you want. Take off your coat and relax.

(He puts down his serving tray to pick up casket, holding out other

THE VENETIAN TWINS

hand for TONININO's coat. On next speech: TONINO puts tray in BRIGHELLA's held-out hand and takes casket back; BRIGHELLA gives him tray and takes back casket. Finally BOTH slam both objects down, fold arms and glare. Then TONINO snatches casket.)

TONINO. No thanks, old man, not me. But I don't want you to think I'm trying to cheat you out of your tip; here's a half ducat. *(Gives him a coin.)*

BRIGHELLA. I'm really awful much obliged to you, sir. The Bisognosis always was a generous bunch. The gentleman your brother in Venice, now he was the most generous of them all.
TONINO. *(Aside.)* Still going on about my brother in Venice! *(To BRIGHELLA, giving him another coin.)* Just when was it you knew my brother in Venice?
BRIGHELLA. It would have been about two years ago —
TONINO. *(Giving him another coin.)* Two years ago? What do you mean, two years ago?
BRIGHELLA. Well, y'see sir, it's cause I happened to be in Venice —

(PANCRAZIO comes in.)

PANCRAZIO. Brighella, Miss Rosaura's calling for you.
BRIGHELLA. Be right there.
TONINO. First finish what you were saying about Venice, old fellow.
PANCRAZIO. Sorry, sir, but she needs him now. Get a move on!
BRIGHELLO. See you later, Signor Zanetto, sir.

(BRIGHELLO goes out.)

TONINO. *(Aside.)* Damn his interference! I'm dying to find out about this.
PANCRAZIO. A pleasure to see you again, Mr. Zanetto.
TONINO. Always an honor, sir.
PANCRAZIO. [But I feel terribly sorry for you: It seems from

the look on your face that you didn't take my advice.

TONINO. Oh, no, I'm eager to hear any advice a gentleman like you has to give.

PANCRAZIO. Hear it, but not follow it, is that the idea?

TONINO. What makes you say so?

PANCRAZIO. That's how it seems to me, but maybe I'm wrong.] I see you here in this house, and I don't know what to think.

TONINO. *(Aside.)* Let's see, maybe this fellow knows what goes on here. *(To PANCRAZIO.)* You think the people in this house are up to no good?

PANCRAZIO. Oh, no doubt of it!

TONINO. Out for everything they can get?

PANCRAZIO. And in every way!

TONINO. This Professor seems to be an especially shady character.

PANCRAZIO. Mm. *(Makes a noncommittal, but affirmative gesture.)*

TONINO. But the girl, now, what do you think of her?

PANCRAZIO. Don't trust her, you'll see, don't trust her. She's totally corrupt.

TONINO. What, with that sweet, sad little face?

PANCRAZIO. Ah, my friend, the ones who look the most demure always have the worst vices to conceal.

TONINO. You realize what an awful thing you're saying?

PANCRAZIO. And yet it's the truth.

TONINO. But in that case, sir, what are you doing here with all these dangerous types?

PANCRAZIO. I keep trying to teach them to change their ways; but all my efforts lead nowhere. It's no use,[it's no use.]

TONINO. It would be wonderful if you could save them.

PANCRAZIO. But instead they always seem to go from bad to worse.

TONINO. Still, the young girl doesn't seem so bad.

PANCRAZIO. She could make a stone fall in love with her; but God help the man she has her eye on!

TONINO. She was asking me to think about marriage.

PANCRAZIO. Good grief! Marriage? What a terrifying word!

TONINO. What's so terrifying about marriage? In some ways it's

THE VENETIAN TWINS 53

the most beautiful word you'll find in any dictionary.

PANCRAZIO. But don't you remember, marriage is like a lead weight that makes you sweat all day and all night? It weighs on your spirit, it weighs on your body, it weighs on your wallet?

TONINO. Marriage only weighs a man down if he isn't thinking right. Weighs down your spirit? Not true. The love of a good wife is the sweetest and most lasting love in the world, as free of lust as it is of anger or bitterness. [It comforts your heart, raises your spirits, and guarantees that you'll be a happy husband, sharing with your wife all your pleasures and your assets.] Then you say marriage weighs down your body? Not true. A wife frees her husband from stress. She runs the house, orders the meals, supervises the servants. [She uses her natural instinct for thrift and organization to keep the household economy in order, which saves money.] Then does marriage weigh down your wallet? Not true at all. The man who's inclined to spend money will spend less outside, because he's got a house to keep up. [And if he spends it on his wife, it does him honor in the long run, because his wife and his house look finer and happier. If the wife has some sense, she can make do with very little. If she's greedy and hard to please, the husband has to be reasonable himself, to teach her how. And if she ruins him with debts, it's not the wife's fault, it's his own willingness to go along. So does marriage weigh on your mind? It's just not true, whether the wife is an honest woman or not. If she's honest, you can trust her; if she's dishonest, you can always cure her with a good beating; it's a wonderful way to teach women discretion.] In other words, marriage is a good thing if you're good, and a wicked thing only if you're wicked. As the Venetian poet says:

If you're steady, calm and wise

Marriage blossoms in your eyes

Those for whom it's always bad

Are old, or impotent, or mad.

PANCRAZIO. *(Aside.)* He's not the idiot I thought he was. *(To TONINO.)* But don't you remember that a woman is a witch and a Circe, who lures men on only to cheat them, and loves only for her own profit?

TONINO. Really? I'm sorry, but that's just a lot of nonsense. [Women aren't all poured from one mold. There may be a lot of bad ones, but there are many more good ones, the same as with men. A woman is a witch? Not true at all.] Did you ever see the trick a toad plays to catch a nightingale? All it does is hide in a ditch with its mouth turned aside. The nightingale comes by, it's attracted to the toad's neck, pulls at it, pulls again, and gets so twisted up the toad can swallow it with no problem. Whose fault is that — the toad's or the nightingale's? And men are the same way. We see a woman, we go after her; we fall under her spell. Whose fault is that? Ours! Women don't have any power to make us run in circles around them; if they control us, it's our own weakness that lets them; [they turn arrogant only because we flatter them].

PANCRAZIO. *(Aside.)* I'm not getting anywhere with him this time! *(To TONINO.)* Signor Zanetto, I don't know what to say. If you want Miss Rosaura so much, take her, but think carefully first.

TONINO. I didn't say I wanted her. I was talking about marriage in general; [I never said I wanted to get married. I was talking about women in general;] I never said a word about Rosaura. [I can't decide if she's fish or fowl.] I like her, and I don't like her. I can't make up my mind, and what you've said makes me suspicious. So I've decided not to do anything for the moment.

PANCRAZIO. That's a very wise decision. Three cheers for you. You're a real gentleman.

TONINO. Well, you seem to be a decent fellow yourself, so let me tell you a little secret.

PANCRAZIO. Say whatever you like. You can count on me not to tell a soul.

TONINO. You see this casket?

PANCRAZIO. Are those jewels?

TONINO. Yes indeed.

PANCRAZIO. Let me see. *(Looking in box.)* Beautiful, very beautiful.

TONINO. I got them by pure chance, from some poor lunatic in a patchwork coat. I don't know who he was, but his master, whom they belong to, must be going crazy hunting for them. Since I'm heading on my way, I thought I might hand them over to you, so that you might find the man and give them back to him.

PANCRAZIO. This shows great consideration on your part. You are truly a man of honor.

TONINO. Any gentleman would have done the same.

THE VENETIAN TWINS

PANCRAZIO. But what if a long time goes by, and I search everywhere, but I still can't find the owner? What should I do with them?

TONINO. Use them as dowries for orphan girls.

PANCRAZIO. You Venetians are generous men.

TONINO. As gentlemen of rank, we have to do all the good we can. Think of all the miserable poor people who have to live on charity. It's true that some rich people are only generous, as they say, out of self-interest; but there are just as many who give out of the goodness of their hearts. That's how I am: I'd destroy my own fortune to save a friend, and I'd give women the shirt off my back.

(TONINO goes out.)

PANCRAZIO. This time self-interest comes first. I'll use these jewels to bait my trap. If Rosaura wants them, she'll have to pay for them, at a price that means little to her and everything to me.

(PANCRAZIO goes out.)

Scene 3

(Street near the inn.
ARLECCHINO comes out of the inn, followed by ZANETTO.)

ARLECCHINO. *(At the inn door, arguing with ZANETTO.)* You amaze me. I'm an honest man. I gave *you* the jewels and the money.

ZANETTO. That's a flat lie. You're a swindler. You never gave me a thing.

ARLECCHINO. *(Walking away in a huff.)* You lie like a rug and I hope you slip on it.

ZANETTO. *(Running after him.)* Thief, murderer, give me back my jewels. I want my jewels.

ARLECCHINO. I told you, I already gave them to you.

ZANETTO. Dirty dog! My jewels, my money, all my things!

ARLECCHINO. You've gone completely crazy.

ZANETTO. You robbed me, you killed me.

ARLECCHINO. Keep away from me or I will kill you!

(CONSTABLE comes in, [followed by GUARDS.])

CONSTABLE. What's all this about? Who's been robbed? Where's the thief?
ZANETTO. That's him right there, my valet. He was supposed to bring me a casket of jewels and money from Bergamo, and he stole every cent of it from me and killed me.
ARLECCHINO. It's all a complete lie. I'm an honest man.
CONSTABLE. [*(To GUARDS, indicating ARLECCHINO.)* Chain him up and take him to the jailhouse.
ARLECCHINO. But] I didn't do it!
CONSTABLE. If that's true, then you won't have any problem getting out.
ARLECCHINO. But in that case why do I have to go in?
CONSTABLE. You just have to. Now come on, don't make it worse on yourself.
ARLECCHINO. God damn it! This is all your fault, you halfwit, you cretin! But you'll pay for this when I get out!

[(GUARDS lead him away.)]

CONSTABLE. Sir, if you think he's really the thief, file a complaint and the judge will decide. Meantime, I'll put in my report and make note of the charges. If you have any evidence, register it at the Criminal Court office.

(The CONSTABLE goes out. If there are no GUARDS, he takes ARLECCHINO with him.)

ZANETTO. I don't know what he just said. I didn't understand a word of it. All I wanted was to get my jewels back. The ones my rich uncle gave me, [the ones he told me over and over again he brought with him from Venice when he took me to live in Bergamo.]
BEATRICE. *(Coming in and seeing ZANETTO.)* My dearest, have mercy on me.
ZANETTO. *(Aside.)* Eyes of fire — a mouth full of poison!

THE VENETIAN TWINS 57

BEATRICE. For pity's sake, don't go. All I ask is one little favor: Just listen to me for a moment. I'm on my knees before you. [Look at my tears and show some mercy.]

ZANETTO. *(Holding one hand towards BEATRICE's eyes.)* I don't feel her eyes burning me. I'm sure there's no fiery flames there.

BEATRICE. Only hear me out, and you'll be glad you did.

ZANETTO. *(Aside.)* And her little mouth is so pretty I wouldn't mind being poisoned by it.

BEATRICE. Remember, I've risked my life and honor for your sake.

ZANETTO. For me?

BEATRICE. *(Rising from her knees.)* Yes, for you. I love you more than my own soul. For you, the one image always in my mind and heart.

ZANETTO. You like me that much?

BEATRICE. Yes, I love you, I adore you; you are my soul.

ZANETTO. *(Aside.)* Is that a demon talking? If it is, it's a damn pretty one!

BEATRICE. My love can't stand to wait any longer. Come, give me your hand [and tell me we'll be married.

ZANETTO. *(Aside.)* Oh, this is just what I like. No ritual and no ceremony.

BEATRICE. Don't make me suffer any longer, come!

ZANETTO. Miss, I'm here. Tell me what to do.

BEATRICE. Give me your hand.]

ZANETTO. You can have them both if you want. *(Takes her hand.)* Oh, darling! Oh, what a hand! Like satin, like silk!

FLORINDO. *(Coming in and seeing them; aside.)* What am I seeing? Tonino's found Beatrice! What rotten luck I have! Let's see if I can break this up.

BEATRICE. And here's just the man to be our witness.

ZANETTO. You think the gentleman will do?

BEATRICE. Of course. At last, Signor Florindo, my fiancé and I are safe in each other's arms. He's ready to take my hand in marriage, and we hope that you are ready to be our witness.

ZANETTO. Yes, signor, be our witness.

FLORINDO. That's something I never really like to do, but I'll do anything for a friend. *(To ZANETTO.)* But first, if I could have a

word with you.
ZANETTO. Gladly. *(To BEATRICE.)* Don't go away, I'll be back in an instant.
FLORINDO. *(Softly, to ZANETTO.)* My friend, tell me, weren't you just in that house over there? *(Points to PROFESSOR's house.)*
ZANETTO. Yes indeed, signor.
FLORINDO. And if you don't mind my asking, what were you doing there?
ZANETTO. I was there to marry the Professor's daughter.
FLORINDO. And now you want to marry Miss Beatrice?
ZANETTO. Yes indeed, signor.
FLORINDO. But aren't you engaged to Miss Rosaura?
ZANETTO. Oh, well, that's no problem, I'll marry them both. *(To BEATRICE.)* I'm all yours.
FLORINDO. No, stop, this can't be right. You're joking.
ZANETTO. Not at all. I could marry half a dozen more.
FLORINDO. Where do you think we are, Turkey? I'm amazed at you. You know perfectly well that you can't marry more than one of them.
ZANETTO. Why not?
FLORINDO. Because you made a promise to the Professor's daughter, just now, there in her house. If you go back on your word, they can put you in prison, and it'll cost you everything you've got.
ZANETTO. *(Aside.)* Hell! *(To BEATRICE.)* I've changed my mind.
BEATRICE. What do you mean?
ZANETTO. Sorry, I've got to have my hand back.
BEATRICE. But I don't understand.
ZANETTO. Doesn't matter if you understand or not. What's done is done.
BEATRICE. But — how can you treat me this way?
ZANETTO. I'm sorry. I've never been to prison. And I don't want to go there.
BEATRICE. What do you mean, prison?
ZANETTO. It turns out I can't marry two of you. The other one's a Professor's daughter. And I promised her. So if I marry you she'd put me in prison. *(Going out.)* See you.

(ZANETTO goes.)

THE VENETIAN TWINS

BEATRICE. I'm so unhappy! My Tonino's gone insane. The way he talks I don't even recognize him.

FLORINDO. Miss Beatrice, please let me explain. Tonino has fallen in love with this girl Rosaura, Professor Balanzoni's daughter, and has promised to marry her. As a result, he has gone a little bit insane, torn between love and guilt.

BEATRICE. Oh, Lord! Can this really be true?

FLORINDO. Only too true. If you don't believe me, look at the way he talked to you just now.

BEATRICE. I said I could hardly recognize him.

FLORINDO. So what will you do?

BEATRICE. If Tonino leaves me, I only want to die.

(LELIO comes in and sees them.)

FLORINDO. Remember that even if Tonino leaves you, Florindo is still here for you.

LELIO. If Tonino leaves you, there's a hero ready to avenge the wrong he's done you.

FLORINDO. I'll always be faithful to you.

LELIO. I'll take you to seventh heaven.

FLORINDO. [I come from a noble family.

LELIO. I come from a long line of great men.

FLORINDO. I can bring you the good things of life.

LELIO. I own gold mines; I can bring you anything you want.

FLORINDO. I'm sure you don't find me unattractive.

LELIO. I'm sure you find me one of nature's masterpieces.

FLORINDO. Please, Miss Beatrice, pay no attention to that conceited cartoon over there.

LELIO. Don't listen to that underfed, underbred little sissy.]

FLORINDO. I'm yours if you want me.

LELIO. Say the word, and you're mine.

TONINO. *(Entering and seeing them; aside.)* What's this! Beatrice — and the two of them fighting over her —

FLORINDO. [Speak to me, dearest.

TONINO. *(Aside.)* Dearest!

LELIO. Open your ruby lips, my beauty.

TONINO. *(Aside.)* My beauty! This is getting out of hand.]

60 THE VENETIAN TWINS

FLORINDO. If Tonino leaves you, he's a traitor.

LELIO. If Tonino leaves you, he's a bastard.

TONINO. *(Plunging into the fray, sword drawn.)* Tonino's no traitor, and by God, he's no bastard! Tonino would never desert Beatrice. *(To FLORINDO.)* [You deceitful creature, you take my breath away.] Fine friend you are, you two-faced little pipsqueak!

FLORINDO. But Miss Rosaura —

TONINO. What Miss Rosaura? You shut up, you little lump of stucco! You tell everyone my name, and now you want to tell the world everything I do? From now on you keep my name out of your mouth, and don't come near me unless you want your belly to look like Swiss cheese.

LELIO. And what about me?

TONINO. And what about you, you little caricature? [If you're smart, you're on your way. If not, well,] I got you down in our first match; in the next one I'll cut your heart out. *(Taking BEATRICE's hand.)* This woman's mine and that's the story.

BEATRICE. You say that I'm yours, but —

TONINO. Not here, there's too many people watching. Come with me. To hell with those two rusty pepper mills, those windbags, those rolled-up newspapers.

(TONINO goes out with BEATRICE.)

FLORINDO. I'll be revenged or my name's not Florindo.

LELIO. I'm not me if I don't slice that bastard to bits.

FLORINDO. My friend, we've both been insulted.

LELIO. Let's share our revenge.

FLORINDO. Let's go and plan it now.

LELIO. I'm in such a rage I could do something incredible.

FLORINDO. Let's both jump on him swords in hand.

LELIO. No, let's get pistols and shoot him in the back.

FLORINDO. That would be a low trick.

LELIO.
"Let him die fairly, or by treachery
 So long as I am there, his death to see."

(LELIO goes out.)

FLORINDO. Fine words, young Lelio! But thank you, I'll plot my revenge alone. Either Beatrice will be mine, or Tonino will die at the tip of this sword!

(FLORINDO goes out.)

CURTAIN

ACT III

Scene 1

(The street.
PANCRAZIO, carrying the casket, comes in, meeting TIBURZIO, a goldsmith.)

PANCRAZIO. Signor Tiburzio, what luck! I was just on my way to your shop to see you.
TIBURZIO. Ah, Signor Pancrazio, I'm at your service. What can I do for you?
PANCRAZIO. I'll tell you. I have some jewels to sell. [They belonged to a charitable widow, who left them to me to be used as dowries for orphan girls who can't afford to marry.] Could you tell me honestly how much they're worth?
TIBURZIO. Gladly, always ready to do your bidding. Do you have them with you?
PANCRAZIO. Right here, as you can see.

(PANCRAZIO takes out the casket and opens it. The CONSTABLE [and GUARDS,] coming in, notice this and watch them from a distance.)

TIBURZIO. Signor Pancrazio, these jewels look very valuable. I couldn't give an accurate estimate out here on the street. Come to my shop and we'll do it there.
PANCRAZIO. Fine, fine. By the way, some of them are a little tarnished. Do you have anything I could use to clean them?
TIBURZIO. Really, I have my own private mixture. I don't let everyone know about it, because it contains an extremely powerful poison.

PANCRAZIO. No need to worry about telling me. You can be sure I won't misuse it. After all, you know me.

TIBURZIO. I know you're a good and honest man, and I'm glad to help you out. By a stroke of luck, I have a little packet of the powder with me. *(Hands PANCRAZIO a paper packet.)* Here it is, take it, use it, and you'll see the jewels come out all clean and sparkling. Then if you decide to sell them, I may be able to get you a much better price for them.

PANCRAZIO. I'll see that you get a fair share. I'm very grateful to you. See you tomorrow.

TIBURZIO. Always a pleasure.

(TIBURZIO goes out.)

PANCRAZIO. *(Aside.)* [These jewels are really very beautiful. But the settings are very old, and the diamonds are so tarnished I can't tell how good they are. But with this powder they'll be good as new.]

CONSTABLE. *(Watching from a distance; aside.)* That casket of jewels is just like the one that fellow Arlecchino described to us.

PANCRAZIO. *(Aside.)* And I can hope that such a beautiful present will make my darling Rosaura think twice about me.

CONSTABLE. Excuse me, signor, if you don't mind.

PANCRAZIO. What is it? What do you want?

CONSTABLE. Would you hand me those jewels?

PANCRAZIO. Why?

CONSTABLE. They're stolen goods.

PANCRAZIO. What? Signor, I am an honest man.

CONSTABLE. In that case, where did you get them?

PANCRAZIO. From Signor Zanetto Bisognosi.

CONSTABLE. Signor Zanetto Bisognosi tells us they were stolen from him; since you have them, we have to suspect you of the crime.

PANCRAZIO. What, a respectable man like me? Known for my piety?

CONSTABLE. Just be glad you're not under arrest. Bring the jewels to the courthouse, and if you're as innocent as you say, there'll be no problem.

PANCRAZIO. Me in court? Me before a judge? But I'm well

THE VENETIAN TWINS 65

known here. Anyone can tell you I'm no thief. *(ZANETTO comes in.)* Look, here's Signor Zanetto. He can tell you how I got these jewels.

ZANETTO. Jewels? My jewels?

CONSTABLE. Do you know these jewels, Signor Zanetto?

ZANETTO. Yes. Signor, these are the jewels my rich uncle left me. I know them; they're mine.

PANCRAZIO. *(To CONSTABLE.)* You see, he knows them. They used to be his uncle's, then they were his.

CONSTABLE. *(To ZANETTO.)* And you gave them to Signor Pancrazio?

PANCRAZIO. Yes signor, yes, he did, he gave them to me. *(To ZANETTO.)* Isn't that right?

ZANETTO. [I don't know,] I never gave you nothing.

PANCRAZIO. You never gave me anything? I'm amazed at you.

ZANETTO. And I'm amazed at you. These are mine.

PANCRAZIO. Oh, dear God! Do you want to ruin my reputation?

ZANETTO. Ruin anything you want, I don't know nothing about it. *(To CONSTABLE.)* Mister Signor, can I have my jewels back?

PANCRAZIO. God in Heaven! We were in the Professor's house, in Miss Rosaura's room; you gave them to me and you know you did!

ZANETTO. You're lying, you're just making up stories. You told me women have eyes with flames in them, and that's not true neither.

PANCRAZIO. Constable, this man is insane. Give me back those jewels.

CONSTABLE. Whether he's sane or insane, we're taking the jewels to the courthouse, and the judge can decide who gave them to who. [*(To GUARD.)* Go let Arlecchino out of his cell, and bring him to the courthouse under guard.] *(Or, if there is no GUARD:)* I'll go and get Arlecchino ...

[(GUARDS go out.)]

PANCRAZIO. I'll get witnesses. Quick, I've got to find the Professor, Brighella, Miss Rosaura, Colombina, [all of them,] the whole houseful — quick — I've got to — I'm going — wait a second — let's go — my reputation, my reputation!

THE VENETIAN TWINS

ZANETTO. Well, come on, give me back my jewels. I'm going crazy.

CONSTABLE. Come to the courthouse; when the judge says you can have them, they're yours.

ZANETTO. What does the judge have to do with my jewels?

CONSTABLE. I can't give them back unless he says so.

ZANETTO. And what if he doesn't say I can have them?

CONSTABLE. Then you won't get them.

ZANETTO. Then what will you do with them?

CONSTABLE. Whatever the judge says.

ZANETTO. You mean I might never get them back?

CONSTABLE. Maybe not.

ZANETTO. I should have let that old man have them. At least he went to the trouble of stealing them.

CONSTABLE. Are you afraid the judge will steal them now?

ZANETTO. They're mine, and [I don't want to lose them because of him.] I don't see any difference between him stealing them and the judge keeping them.

CONSTABLE. If that's the way you think, you'd better get a lawyer.

ZANETTO. What would a lawyer do?

CONSTABLE. He could make the judge see that the jewels are yours.

ZANETTO. But why do I need a lawyer for that? They're my jewels, and nobody knows that better than me.

CONSTABLE. But the judge might not believe you.

ZANETTO. He won't believe me but he'll believe the lawyer? [He'd rather believe a liar than the truth?]

CONSTABLE. Lawyers have ways of explaining what their clients mean.

ZANETTO. But who pays the lawyer?

CONSTABLE. You do, of course.

ZANETTO. And the judge?

CONSTABLE. He gets a fee for hearing the case.

ZANETTO. And what about you? You get nothing?

CONSTABLE. Are you kidding! Of course I get paid. And all my men.

ZANETTO. So between the judge, the lawyer, you, and the

THE VENETIAN TWINS 67

guards, I can kiss my jewels goodbye.

CONSTABLE. But how else can we live? Everybody has to get his share.

ZANETTO. You all have to get your share, and I get nothing? Fine! Beautiful! I love it! [I'm going back to the mountains. There's no judges, no lawyers, and no constables. What's mine is mine, and nobody tries to cheat me out of it by pretending to do me a favor.] My friend, I don't know what to say. Divide the jewels up any way you want, and if there's any left over for me, let me know, so I can thank you all kindly. Come on, you sneak thieves, come on, why don't you steal my shirt while you're at it, that's all I've got to say. The sheep doesn't care whether the wolf eats it or the butcher slits its throat. And I don't care if I'm robbed by thieves or by the law. Goodbye.

(ZANETTO goes out.)

CONSTABLE. I think he is insane. Either that or he's brilliant. But it doesn't matter. In my job you can put up with anything people say about you, no matter what, the way a python can swallow a horse.

(He goes out. TONINO comes in.)

TONINO. So that's all friendship means to them nowadays. Florindo came to Venice; I treated him like my own brother. [Then I trust him, I put a woman under his care who's the most important thing in my life,] and he stabs me in the back! How can a friend have the gall to do that to you? [If I did such evil things, I'd be afraid the earth would open up and swallow me.] Friendship is the world's most sacred gift. [It's a medicine sent by nature to heal the world; without it we'd be destroyed, annihilated. A man's love for a woman can start as a lower kind of passion. A love for money and things is a sign of our sinful nature. But the love of friends is based on real virtue,] which is why the world seems to think so little of it. [Nobody today takes Damon and Pythias for an ideal; the faithful Achates is an obscure joke.] Nowadays they're only interested in themselves; instead of one true friend, they have an army of flatterers, who follow them around in the hope of getting something from them. And if their luck turns bad, those so-called friends desert them, [ridicule them, and pay back with ingratitude whatever gifts they've received.] As the great poet Ovid said so beautifully: "When fortune smiles on you, your friends are many. Let fortune frown, and look! You haven't any."

LELIO. *(Coming in; aside.)* There's my rival, the lucky man. Let's see if a few friendly words can put him off guard.

TONINO. *(Aside, seeing LELIO.)* Enough; at least I can settle this one's hash.

LELIO. I bow to you, O hero triumphant, pride of Venice, that jewel of the Adriatic.

TONINO. Your servant, O great thunderer of your own magnificence.

LELIO. Forgive me if the articulation of my emphatic syllables disrupts the serenity of your esteemed eardrums.

TONINO. Kindly mute the trumpet of your eloquence before I shove it down your throat, and the drum after it.

LELIO. Your delicately phrased demand drives me to ecstatic delirium.

TONINO. Signor, I never dreamed you could be found anywhere else.

LELIO. Love's poisoned arrows have pierced my impenetrable heart.

TONINO. I feel sure they've done severe damage to your brain as well.

LELIO. Ah, signor, as a noble Venetian, you cannot be blind — to those in need of your help.

TONINO. You need my help? For what?

LELIO. Because I burn with love.

TONINO. And you want my sympathy?

LELIO. Only you can cure my sickness.

TONINO. Really! What planet did you say you come from?

LELIO. The planet of the adventurers, where I was born under the sun of misery and raised in the city of despair.

TONINO. And will die in a home for the insane.

LELIO. I will cut the thread of my labyrinthine discourse with the shears of brevity. I love Beatrice, I long for her, I sigh for her. I rely on your pity, on your unbelievable generosity, to give her to me.

TONINO. I'll cut the cord of my answer with the dagger of frankness: Beatrice is mine, and I'd sooner give you all the treasures

THE VENETIAN TWINS

of the Ganges than a glimpse of the beauteous beauties of my adored beauty.
(Aside.) Damn it, if he doesn't shut up he'll drive me crazy too.

LELIO. You've murdered me.
TONINO. That's one less lunatic.
LELIO. Ingrate!
TONINO. Loudmouth!
LELIO. Bully!
TONINO. Goddamn halfwit!
LELIO. [If my love drives me mad, beware my madness.
TONINO. Aim the blazing arrows of your bestial madness at me, and you'll strike impenetrable rock.]
LELIO. I'm leaving —
TONINO. Go!
LELIO. I'm leaving —
TONINO. Well, go then!
LELIO. I'm leaving, you vicious—
TONINO. Go before I [chase you off!]
LELIO. I'm leaving, yes, but to go and plot my revenge, and I'll have it before the sun touches the horizon.

(LELIO goes out.)

TONINO. When they're born like that, there's no curing them. Stupid little donkey! [If he'd stayed a minute longer, I'd have gone round the bend with him. Really, everyone in the world is a little crazy, and the ones who think they aren't are the craziest of all. But that one's the cream of the lunatic crop.]

(TONINO is about to go off when PANCRAZIO comes in, bringing BRIGHELLA from the PROFESSOR's house.)

PANCRAZIO. Come along, come along to the courthouse. You've got to testify that I'm innocent.
BRIGHELLA. Looky, there's Signor Zanetto.
PANCRAZIO. *(To TONINO.)* You! How could you deny to my face that you gave me those jewels?
TONINO. Why, it's true. I did give them to you.

PANCRAZIO. *(To BRIGHELLA.)* You see? He admits it. Just tell that to the judge.

TONINO. What does the judge have to do with it?

PANCRAZIO. [Fine work you've done! Making a mess of my reputation!

TONINO. *(Aside.)* What's this; maybe he's found out who owns those jewels.] *(To PANCRAZIO.)* Surely no one thinks they were stolen?

PANCRAZIO. That's just what they do think. And you started it all.

TONINO. My dear signor, I did what I thought best.

PANCRAZIO. What you thought best was worst; you've ruined me.

ARLECCHINO. *(Coming in.)* Well, at least I'm out of there.

TONINO. And here's the one who gave me the jewels.

ARLECCHINO. I gave you the jewels?

TONINO. Yes, you gave them to me.

ARLECCHINO. And the money too?

TONINO. And the money too.

ARLECCHINO. Then why did you tell them I didn't? [You have some nerve, playing a dirty trick like that!]

TONINO. [I'm amazed.] I never told anyone any such thing. You practically forced me to take the money and the jewels. What could I do? I took them. I'm an honest man, I didn't need them, and even if I did, I'd die sooner than steal. I no longer have the jewels. I gather they're in court. [Get them back and you can do what you want with them.] Your money doesn't belong to me and I don't want it. You gave it to me, and here it is back. [An honest man knows his reputation is worth more than all the money in the world. Money comes and goes, but you can't get back your honor, once you've lost it. Take your moneybag. I throw it away, just to show you how little gold and silver mean to me.] You could put all the fine gold in the world into that bag, and it still wouldn't mean as much to me as the honest reputation of the Bisognosi family, for which I'd gladly die, the way Cicero and Cato died for Rome.

(TONINO goes out.)

ARLECCHINO. *(Singing.)* He's gone crazy!

THE VENETIAN TWINS

BRIGHELLA. You can say that again. Anybody who throws money away like that! I'm going to follow him and see what he does.

(BRIGHELLA goes out after TONINO.)

PANCRAZIO. *(Picking up moneybag.)* I'll just take care of this till Zanetto has one of his lucid intervals. Come with me to the courthouse, friend, so we can get back the jewels.
ARLECCHINO. You know what I think? I want to go back to the mountains of Bergamo.
PANCRAZIO. Why?
ARLECCHINO. Because the air in this city drives people crazy.

(ARLECCHINO goes out.)

PANCRAZIO. The whole world breathes the same air. You can find crazy people wherever you go. Some are crazy with conceit, some out of stupidity, some with pride, some with greed. I'm crazy for love, and I suspect that my madness is the greatest of them all.

(PANCRAZIO goes out.)

ZANETTO. *(Coming in.)* Love, I tell you, love is a great thing. The minute I saw Miss Rosaura, I felt myself sizzling like a lamb chop. I can't go on if I don't see her, and talk to her. I've got to find her, and see if we can't get married after all.

(ZANETTO knocks on the PROFESSOR's door.)

ROSAURA. *(Appearing at the upstairs window.)* Signor Zanetto, is that you?
ZANETTO. Oh, you beautiful creature. Shall I come up?
ROSAURA. No, signor, my father says you mustn't.
ZANETTO. Why not?
ROSAURA. Because you said he was my pimp.
ZANETTO. You think I would say a horrible thing like that? [I thought we were going to be husband and wife.]
ROSAURA. But my father showed me the letter.

ZANETTO. The letter I wrote him? Well, good.

ROSAURA. So you admit you wrote it, and then you say you never wrote asking for my hand in marriage?

ZANETTO. I didn't say anything about marriage. I said we would do what we had to do on the spot.

ROSAURA. I don't always understand you. Sometimes you're just too silly for words, and sometimes you're too smart.

ZANETTO. Oh, look, let me come up. [Don't you want me to?] I'm getting a crick in my neck.

ROSAURA. No, you mustn't come up here.

ZANETTO. Then why don't you come down?

ROSAURA. That's worse. Imagine if I were seen talking to you in the street!

ZANETTO. Do you want me to die?

ROSAURA. You poor thing! Your passion isn't going to kill you anytime soon.

ZANETTO. You don't believe me? When I'm away from you I feel like a fish out of water. I babble, I see things, I'm completely out of my mind. If you don't help me, if you don't give me your hand, I'll keel over and die right in front of you, a lump of dead meat at your door, ready to be cooked in the fire of your cruelty.

ROSAURA. [What witty metaphors!] Tell me more, what else do you feel?

ZANETTO. What do I feel? How can I feel anything, with you up there and me down here? If you want to feel something nice, either come down here or let me come up there. I promise to behave myself.

ROSAURA. But can't you behave yourself at this distance?

ZANETTO. I'm sorry, at this distance I can't do anything.

ROSAURA. But what would you do if you were closer?

ZANETTO. What would I do? What would I do? I can't say it, it's too embarrassing. I'll sing it in a little song if you want.

ROSAURA. Oh, I'd love to hear you sing.

ZANETTO. *(Sings; if desired, ARLECCHINO and BRIGHELLA can appear upstage, playing or miming accompaniment.)*

IF I COULD JUST BE NEAR YOU
MY DARLING LITTLE MISS
THEN FROM YOUR PRETTY LIPS
I'D STEAL A LITTLE SOMETHING

THE VENETIAN TWINS

TO SEE YOU AND TO HEAR YOU
SO CLOSE WOULD BE SUCH BLISS
AND YOU'D FORGIVE MY SLIPS
IF I SHOULD SAY A DUMB THING

BUT I BEGIN TO FEAR YOU
WILL NEVER GRANT ME THIS
YOUR DAINTY FINGERTIPS
WILL KEEP ME AT A DISTANCE

IF YOU ARE TOO SEVERE, YOU
WILL CHILL ME LIKE A SWISS
BECAUSE MY ARDOR DIPS
THE MORE YOU SHOW RESISTANCE

SO BE A LITTLE DEAR, YOU,
AND SPARE ME THIS NEAR MISS
JUST SHAKE YOUR PRETTY HIPS
AND I'LL COME UPSTAIRS RUSHING

TO WORSHIP AND REVERE YOU
CARESS AND HUG AND KISS
AND TAKE SUCH WONDROUS TRIPS
TO — OH, YOU'VE GOT ME BLUSHING!

ROSAURA. Bravo, that's wonderful!

(She applauds; so do ARLECCHINO and BRIGHELLA, if they are present.)

ZANETTO. Did you like it? I'm ready if you are.
ROSAURA. But I wish you could explain something I don't understand. You seem to behave like two entirely different people. Sometimes you seem stupid; other times you're a witty young man. Sometimes you're horribly rude, and sometimes you're almost shy. Why do you keep changing this way?
ZANETTO. I didn't know I did that — I mean, in my heart I'm not always so sure — I mean, when I look in your eyes — I mean,

well, Miss, it's how I am.

ROSAURA. Now you see, that was all complete nonsense.

ZANETTO. *(Attempting to climb wall to balcony.)* But I know what I mean when I say it. I just can't explain myself. If you'd let me up there, I could explain myself much better.

ROSAURA. You know what I think about the way you talk? I think you're just leading me on, and you don't really love me at all.

BEATRICE. *(Enters[, with her SERVANT], stopping when she sees ZANETTO. Aside.)* Tonino talking to a young girl? I must listen!

ZANETTO. I love you so much; without you I'm like a bird without a nest, a rooster without a hen, a stallion without a mare, a little pig without his own little sow. It's true, darling, I love you, I want to throw myself in the ocean of your beauty and drown, I want to splash around in your sweetness like a water bird in a lake, I want to stir up the dust of your affection, like, um, like a donkey kicking up sand in the desert

ROSAURA. *(Aside.)* I think he's starting to get weirder than ever.

BEATRICE. *(Coming in between ZANETTO and his view of ROSAURA.)* You traitor! You ingrate! You liar! This is how you keep your vow of fidelity? You just promised to marry me, and now you betray me? This is the third time you've fed me the same lie! Look at me, you monster, look me in the eye, if you can bear to do so. [But no, you're blushing, you're covered with shame, shaking with fright at my anger. You low creature! Heartless fiend! Filthy liar!] Why did you lure me from my father's house? Make me desert my homeland? Why did you swear you'd marry me, if your heart belonged to another woman? If someone had told me you were so evil, I would never have believed it. But now I've seen the truth with my own eyes, the truth of my shame, my betrayal, my humiliation. I'll never trust you again. I no longer love you. You savage, I release you from your promise, and leave you to your fate. [Your love is nothing to me, your claim on me has vanished, your future no longer concerns me.] But wait and see, your treacherous heart won't go its merry way forever, you will be paid back in kind. Yes, you brute, you savage, love my rival, worship her beauty, so superior to mine, but never dream that another woman will endure you, trust you, love you, half as much as I once did!

THE VENETIAN TWINS 75

(BEATRICE runs off [followed by her SERVANT]. ZANETTO has listened to her speech attentively and with great interest. As soon as she is gone, he turns back to ROSAURA.)

ZANETTO. So, to get back to what I was saying —
ROSAURA. You mean, to the lies you were telling me, you hypocrite! How could you promise her all those things, and then come and try to cheat me? No, you scoundrel, you cheat, I won't let you! Love the woman you promised to love! Go and make up for the dishonesty in your heart. Wait, wait, I'll show you how much I don't love you, how much I even hate you and despise you. I'm going to get the letter you wrote my father begging to marry me, you deceitful man, and then you'll see that you can't lie to Rosaura!

(ROSAURA disappears from window.)

ZANETTO. *(Calling after her.)* I'm sure it'll be all right when we're married. *(Seeing she's gone.)* This one calls me "scoundrel," the other one says "brute." This one "cheat," that one "savage." What else can go wrong? Poor Zanetto! I'm desperate They all hate me. Nobody loves me. I'll never get married. [If I had a rope, I'd hang myself. If I had a knife, I'd cut my throat. If I saw a river, I'd drown myself. The women fight over me in jealousy, and I'm caught between them, I don't get to put a word in.] Any of you women out there want me? I'm not all that ugly. No, I can tell, nobody wants me, they all attack me, they all hate me. It's all because I'm so handsome, I curse my good looks, and my miserable fate!

(ZANETTO goes out.)

ROSAURA. *(Coming back to the window.)* Look, look, here's that letter! — Oh, the coward's run away. Silly of me to think he'd wait. His shame and embarrassment drove him off. But I'll find him and I'll get my revenge. *(TONINO comes in.)* Wait — here he is again. You have the gall to show yourself in my sight, you beast? You're incorrigible! Here's your letter — look at what I've done to it. *(Tears the letter into bits and throws it at him.)* There! I've thrown it

76   **THE VENETIAN TWINS**

to the winds. And I wish I could tear up your faithless heart the same way.

(ROSAURA disappears from the window. TONINO, who has been looking up at her in astonished silence, gathers up the pieces of the letter.)

BEATRICE. *(Coming in with a letter in her hand[, followed by her SERVANT].)* I've finally found your letter, you vile scoundrel. There it is, traitor. Now watch, and see what I think of you. *(Tears up the letter and throws it on the ground.)* And I wish I could do the same to that little lump of treachery in your chest.

(BEATRICE goes out[, followed by her SERVANT].)

TONINO. *(Picking up the pieces of the second letter, fitting them together, and comparing the two as he speaks.)* What's going on here? What is this all about? It's certainly a new twist. Two women throwing their torn-up letters at me. I've never written to Rosaura, and I've certainly never been unfaithful to Beatrice. So either they're both insane, or there must be something fishy going on. Let's see what's in these two letters. *(Looks at BEATRICE's, assembling the pieces.)* "I hereby promise ... to Miss Beatrice etcetera and so forth ... Signed, Antonio Bisognosi." Fine. What's in the other one? "This letter will serve as contract ... and so forth ... settlement agreed on ... marriage between ... legitimate heir ... Miss Rosaura Balanzoni ... and Signor Zanetto Bisognosi." What! This is some kind of fraud! I'm not Zanetto. Let's see, when was this drawn up? "Brambana Valley, Bergamo, January 14, 1746." In Bergamo? What is this? Who signed it? "Zanetto Bisognosi his mark." They all do think I'm Zanetto, but nobody would have dared draw this up and sign my name to it. And it's certainly not my writing. So what can this be? Could it have something to do with my brother Zanetto? He does live in Bergamo. It could be. And he might be here in Verona without my knowing it. [That Brighella in the Professor's house, who kept talking about knowing my brother in Venice, made me suspect that he knew I wasn't really Zanetto. And then all the crazy things that have been going

THE VENETIAN TWINS

on would make sense.] Who knows? It could be. Isn't it incredible? I've got to find out. [That old servant in the house will know if it's true or not. I'll test him on it, but without giving myself away. Damn, but it's tricky. I've got to be careful, play it very close to the vest.] *(Pounds on PROFESSOR's door.)* Hello in there!

BRIGHELLA. *(Appearing at the door.)* Your servant, sir. Was that you knocking?

TONINO. Yes, it was me.

BRIGHELLA. I'm sorry, sir, but I've been ordered not to let you in the house.

TONINO. No? Why not?

(Offstage, in the house, we hear ROSAURA scream something incomprehensible, and the PROFESSOR shouting back for her to calm down.)

BRIGHELLA. The mistress is screaming and fainting, and the master's in a fury. If you take my advice, you'll go away[, because if they see you there's no telling what they'll do].

TONINO. But what do they think I've done?

BRIGHELLA. I don't know. I hear them whining about it, but I haven't got a notion why.

(More noise from the house: ROSAURA yelps, PROFESSOR snaps back, clatter of objects thrown and breaking.)

TONINO. Tell me, my friend, didn't you say you knew my brother in Venice?

BRIGHELLA. Indeed I did.

TONINO. Does he look like me?

BRIGHELLA. Like two peas in a pod. I couldn't tell one of you from the other.

TONINO. And you said it's two years since you've seen him?

BRIGHELLA. About two years, yes.

TONINO. My brother —

BRIGHELLA. Yes, sir, that's Signor Tonino.

TONINO. And who do you think I am then?

BRIGHELLA. That's a good one! You're Signor Zanetto.

TONINO. And I came here —

BRIGHELLA. From Bergamo, to marry with Miss Rosaura.

TONINO. Bravo! You know it all, you're a bright fellow. *(Aside.)* Now I understand the whole business.

BRIGHELLA. But tell me, sir, if you don't mind my being nosy, did they ever find out what happened to your sister?

TONINO. Never. So you also know that whole story, about how she disappeared?

BRIGHELLA. Sure thing. Your dear father that's gone now used to tell me that whole story time and again.

TONINO. Poor man, he never got over it. He'd sent her to Bergamo and she vanished on the way, nobody knows how.

BRIGHELLA. What can you do? One less girl to marry off. Well, sir, if you have no orders for me, I'd better get back inside, so they don't spot me talking to you, or I'll catch hell for it. See you later.

(BRIGHELLA goes back into the house.)

TONINO. Your slave for life, friend. Of all the incredible coincidences! Could this be? My brother is in Verona, and our paths have never crossed? [We're being mistaken for each other, and a million confusions have sprung up all in one day.] Now I understand this business with the jewels and the money. [That Arlecchino must be my brother's servant, and thought he was giving those things to him. If I'd known they were my brother's, I'd never have tried to give them back.] I'd really like to see this brother of mine! But that's the story. Now I've just got to keep looking till I find him.

COLOMBINA. *(Coming out of the house; to audience.)* You should hear Miss Rosaura jabbering, the things she says about Signor Zanetto; I can't stand it any longer; it's driving me up the wall.

TONINO. What's wrong, miss? What are you so upset about?

COLOMBINA. Signor, you should know if anyone does. I'm all worked up because I've been taking your side.

TONINO. Taking my side? I'm very grateful. But why should you?

THE VENETIAN TWINS

COLOMBINA. Because Miss Rosaura's gotten all high and mighty, thinking she's some kind of grand lady, and she's just being horrible to everybody.

TONINO. And she's been saying things about me?

COLOMBINA. You wouldn't believe! And because I took your side, and spoke up to defend you, she threw herself on me like a wild beast, ready to claw me to shreds. *(Tidying herself.)* Nasty creature, with her endless jabber; I'd feel sorry for her if I didn't know who she really is.

TONINO. But isn't she the Professor's daughter?

COLOMBINA. She's Miss Nobody from Nowhere, a piece of bad luck straight out of hell. *(Coming up close and confiding it to him as a secret.)* A pilgrim on his way to Rome found her on the road.

TONINO. What? But then why does the Professor call her his daughter?

COLOMBINA. Because the old schemer's another nasty piece of work. He thinks he'll marry her off to some rich young man.

TONINO. [*(Aside.)* I knew there was something shady about that Professor.] *(To COLOMBINA.)* But does Miss Rosaura know she isn't his daughter?

COLOMBINA. She doesn't know, and if he has his way she never will.

TONINO. And how long has the Professor been passing her off as his daughter?

COLOMBINA. Ever since she was a baby in her cradle.

TONINO. And how old is she?

COLOMBINA. She says she's twenty-one, but I don't believe it and neither should you.

TONINO. She can't be much more than that. Tell me something else: Where was this pilgrim coming from?

COLOMBINA. From Venice.

TONINO. And where did he find the little girl?

COLOMBINA. Somewhere in the foothills near Caldiera, between Vicenza and here.

TONINO. Wrapped up in baby clothes?

COLOMBINA. Right, in baby clothes.

TONINO. Did you ever happen to see them?

COLOMBINA. It seems to me the Professor kept them, but I've never seen them myself.

TONINO. But about this pilgrim who found her — could she have been his daughter? Did he say she had a name?

COLOMBINA. She wasn't his daughter; he just found her at the roadside, near where the highwaymen had robbed and killed some coach passengers. [And this little baby had somehow stayed alive by pure chance.] He had no idea what her name might be, so the Professor just named her Rosaura.

TONINO. *(Aside, dashing downstage, away from COLOMBINA.)* Oh, this is lovely! It looks like this could be my sister Flaminia. She was lost between Verona and Vicenza, when they murdered my poor mother, who was bringing her to Bergamo.

COLOMBINA. *(Aside.)* What the hell is he babbling to himself about?

TONINO. *(Coming back to her.)* Do you know if there was a locket pinned to the baby clothes, with a portrait inside of two little boys?

COLOMBINA. I think I once heard the Professor say something about a locket, but why are you asking me all these questions?

TONINO. No more, thanks. I've found out what I need to know. *(Aside.)* This has to be my long-lost sister and no one else. Thank you, God. What an incredible story! Two brothers! And a sister! All here! All together! It's like something from an old comedy.

COLOMBINA. *(Aside.)* It looks like she might really be the daughter of some high-ranking gentleman. *(To TONINO.)* Signor, if Miss Rosaura turns out to be somebody important, promise me in God's name you won't tell her I said all those bad things about her.

TONINO. No, no, you dear girl, don't worry. It's natural for chambermaids to complain about their mistresses. You'd sooner be in jail living on bread and water than not be allowed to grumble now and then.

(TONINO goes out.)

COLOMBINA. There I am, running off at the mouth again, and all I've done is to help Rosaura and put myself in the wrong. That

THE VENETIAN TWINS

strange Signor Zanetto asked me so many questions. And probably all he wants to do is cause even more trouble.

PROFESSOR. *(Appearing in the doorway, with PANCRAZIO.)* Colombina, what are you doing out there on the street?

COLOMBINA. I — I just wanted to see if the vegetable man was coming by.

PROFESSOR. Well, get back in the house, quick, quick.

COLOMBINA. [*(Aside.)* I hope he didn't see Signor Zanetto!]

PROFESSOR. *(As he comes out with PANCRAZIO.)* Get in there, you chatterbox.

COLOMBINA. *(Going in, aside.)* Nasty old grouch!

PROFESSOR. Signor Pancrazio, you're my closest friend in the world. I wanted to tell you that I've made up my mind, in spite of everything that's happened, to go ahead with my daughter's marriage to Signor Zanetto Bisognosi as soon as possible.

PANCRAZIO. What! After she tore up the agreement and threw it in his face, and says she'll never see him again?

PROFESSOR. She did that purely out of jealousy. The plans have gone so far that I can't cancel the marriage without becoming a laughingstock. All of Verona would talk. And then, to be frank, Signor Zanetto is so rich that his bridal gifts alone would guarantee my daughter's future.

PANCRAZIO. Listen to yourself. Greed, greed alone is tempting you to sacrifice this poor innocent dove.

PROFESSOR. Nevertheless, I've made up my mind. And your advice, though I've always valued and trusted it, is not going to make me change my decision, which is decent and dignified, and the best thing for my family.

PANCRAZIO. I warn you, think carefully. Take your time.

PROFESSOR. You yourself have told me, over and over, "There is a tide in the affairs of men." Now please help me, find Signor Zanetto right away, tell him I want them to be married tonight. Please, dear friend, do this for me. I'll see you later.

(The PROFESSOR goes back into the house.)

PANCRAZIO. There's a quick end to all my dreams. The Professor will force her to marry this Venetian fool. And what am I going to do, in my misery? If I tell her I'm mad about her, they won't think me such a good man any more, and I'd lose my best source of income. If she marries that idiot, he'll whisk her right off to Bergamo, and I'll never see her again. I can't let it happen. I'll stoop to any low trick. I'll drop my mask and let the world see me as I am, sooner than lose Rosaura, whom I love more than life itself.

ZANETTO. *(Coming in.)* Signor Pancrazio, I'm desperate.

PANCRAZIO. Death is the consolation of all desperate souls.

ZANETTO. I'm desperate to get married, but nobody wants me. All the women scream insults at me. They hit me and drive me away, like I was a stray dog, a donkey, an animal. Signor Pancrazio, I can't go on, I'm desperate.

PANCRAZIO. Ah, if you'd only done what I said, you wouldn't find yourself in such a miserable state.

ZANETTO. Don't be angry at me! You were so right. I wanted to stay away from women, but I couldn't. I was drawn to them by force, the way a tornado draws water up into the air.

PANCRAZIO. But marriage is wrong for you.

ZANETTO. But why?

PANCRAZIO. I'm convinced that if you got married, you'd be the unhappiest man in the world.

ZANETTO. Then what do you think I should do?

PANCRAZIO. Stay away from women.

ZANETTO. I can't do it.

PANCRAZIO. [Do what I tell you, get out of this city immediately, go back to your home, and you'll be free of all this torture.

ZANETTO. But it'll be the same thing there. The women in Bergamo and the Brambana Valley make fun of me and scream at me too.]

PANCRAZIO. Well, then, what do you want to do?

ZANETTO. I don't know, that's why I'm so desperate.

(ZANETTO pounds his head against the wall.)

PANCRAZIO. If I were in your shoes, do you know what I would do?

THE VENETIAN TWINS

ZANETTO. What?

PANCRAZIO. I'd let death carry me away from all this.

ZANETTO. Death? Dear friend, tell me, isn't there any cure for me other than death?

PANCRAZIO. Death is the only remedy that's guaranteed to cure every illness.

ZANETTO. Look here, you're a decent and honest man, don't you know any little secret that would drive off this crazy need I have to get married?

PANCRAZIO. Let me think. *(Aside.)* He's walked right into my trap. *(To ZANETTO.)* I feel a great sympathy for you. To save you, I'm going to give up part of a rare and valuable treasure I was saving for myself in secret. I have just the medicine you need; I'm the only one who has it, and I always carry it with me in case of another attack. When I was young I was tormented like you, and I'd have gone insane if I didn't have the powder in this little packet. [It's saved me from all the terrible urges of lust; one large dose every five years, and the pains of love disappear, which is why I've lived to this ripe old age. This powder will save your life and free you from every torment.] You just take one pinch of it in a little wine, and you'll find yourself with all passion gone; you can look at women and never blink. You can control them, mock them, revenge yourself for the cruel way they've treated you. Then they'll be desperate for you, but you'll have been cured by this miracle powder, and you'll only laugh at them. [It'll pay them back, in plenty, for the terrible way they've treated you.]

ZANETTO. It sounds incredible! Oh, this is just what I need! For the love of God, Signor Pancrazio, please, give me some of that powder, quick!

PANCRAZIO. But ... it's a great sacrifice ... for me to give this up.

ZANETTO. I'll give you as much money as you want.

PANCRAZIO. Oh, no, money doesn't interest me at all, and to prove it, I'll gladly give you a bit of this powder as a gift. Drink it in a glass of wine, and you'll be cured instantly. At first, you might feel a little flutter in your stomach, and you might think you're dying, but that stops very quickly, and you'll find yourself a new man, you'll be happy and bless me a thousand times over.

84   **THE VENETIAN TWINS**

ZANETTO. Signor, I bless you and thank you already. Don't make me wait, give it to me now.
PANCRAZIO. *(Aside.)* Tiburzio's poison is just the thing to help me get this nitwit away from my Rosaura. *(To ZANETTO, giving him the packet.)* Here's the powder, now you just need some wine.
ZANETTO. I'll go home and drink it there.
PANCRAZIO. *(Aside.)* He might change his mind. *(To ZANETTO.)* No, no, wait right here. I'll go and get you some. *(Aside.)* I feel sorry for him, but it's either his life or my love.

(PANCRAZIO goes into the PROFESSOR's house.)

ZANETTO. I can't go on living the way I am. Whenever I see a woman, I start to burn from head to toe, and then they all make fun of me, or scream at me. The mean things! But now they'll come to me, they'll chase after me, and I'll ignore them, firm as a rock. That'll show them. I can't wait to get my revenge on that slut Rosaura. *(PANCRAZIO comes out of the house with a goblet of wine.)* Here he is again. Did you bring it?
PANCRAZIO. Here's the wine. Put the powder in it.
ZANETTO. *(Doing so.)* Like this?
PANCRAZIO. Perfect. Now drink it. But promise you won't tell anybody that I gave you the secret.
ZANETTO. Don't worry.
PANCRAZIO. Quick.
ZANETTO. I'm ready. Strong as a fortress.

(ZANETTO raises goblet in a toast and is about to drink.)

PANCRAZIO. *(Stopping him.)* And if it hurts a little, bear with it.
ZANETTO. I'll bear with anything.

(ZANETTO starts to drink again. PANCRAZIO, nervous, stops him.)

PANCRAZIO. I'll leave you. Otherwise people might suspect I gave it to you, and then they'd never leave me alone. You know how they are.

THE VENETIAN TWINS

ZANETTO. You're so right.
PANCRAZIO. Oh, won't we laugh at those silly women!
ZANETTO. All of them after me. And I won't care.
PANCRAZIO. Not a bit! Fierce as a lion.
ZANETTO. Will they cry?
PANCRAZIO. And how!
ZANETTO. And I won't care.
PANCRAZIO. Not a bit.
ZANETTO. I'm drinking it.
PANCRAZIO. Quick.
ZANETTO. To your health!

(ZANETTO raises goblet in a toast, then drinks down half its contents at one gulp.)

PANCRAZIO. *(Aside.)* What's done is done!

(PANCRAZIO goes out.)

ZANETTO. *(Drinking gulp by gulp.)* Oh, what a taste! Oh, it's disgusting! Oh, what poison! Oh, my stomach's burning up! What is this stuff? I can't stand to drink any more of it. *(Puts down the goblet.)* Oh, I feel awful. I'm dying, I'm dying, but it's nothing. The powder's working, that's all. If I want all the women to be crazy for me, I've got to put up with it. That's what Signor Pancrazio said ... but ...Oh, God ... I feel awful ... no more girls ... I can't go on ... I shouldn't have drunk it. I won't drink any more ... oh, poor me ... a little water ... water ... water ... *(Staggering around stage, he either collides with an upstage wall or nearly walks off edge of apron.)* I can't see any more ... the earth's shaking under me ... my legs won't hold me up ... oh, my heart ... oh, my heart ... *(Making a last stand center stage.)* Be strong, Zanetto, strong, so the women will run after you ... and you ... you'll make fun of them ... oh, what agony! ... I can't stand up ... I'm falling ... I'm dying ...

(ZANETTO collapses on the ground.)

COLOMBINA. *(Coming out of the house and seeing him.)* What

am I seeing! Mr. Zanetto on the ground? What is it? What's happened? What have you done?

ZANETTO. *(Aside.)* There ... it works ... the women are running after me ...

COLOMBINA. *O dio mio*! He's foaming at the mouth! He must be deathly ill. The poor thing! I've got to get help. [I don't know what else to do for him!]

(COLOMBINA runs back into the house.)

ZANETTO. You see ... she's fallen in love with me ... she's desperate ... *(Staggering up onto his knees.)* and I'm firm as a rock ... but ... oh, God, I'm scared ... I'm dying ... I'm dying ... Help ... help ...

(ZANETTO falls back onto ground.)

FLORINDO. *(Coming in.)* What is this! Tonino on the ground? Now I'll have my revenge.

ZANETTO. *(Writhes, trying to get up.)* Here's another girl running after me ...

FLORINDO. *(Aside, leaning his sword against wall and going to help ZANETTO.)* He's delirious.

ZANETTO. I'm dying ... I'm dying ...

FLORINDO. *(Aside, feeling his pulse.)* He really is dying. *(To ZANETTO.)* But what happened?

ZANETTO. I'm dying ...

FLORINDO. How? Why? ... [Who did this?] *(Aside.)* Even if he's my rival, I pity him.

ZANETTO. I drank it ... I did ... the women ... Signor Pancrazio ... oh, God ... oh, God ... I'm poisoned ... I'm dead ... no ... go away, women ... strong ... hard as a rock, you'll see ... oh, God.

(ZANETTO gives a climactic shudder and dies in FLORINDO's arms.)

FLORINDO. *(Looking around in confusion.)* The poor creature's dead. But who killed him? [What did he die of?] What's this? A gob-

THE VENETIAN TWINS

let of wine. *(Picks it up and looks at it.)* It's all cloudy, there's something in it. The poor man was poisoned.

(FLORINDO puts goblet back on ground.)

COLOMBINA. *(Hurrying out of the house, with PROFESSOR.)* Quick, sir, come quick and help this poor young man.
PROFESSOR. Hurry, Brighella, get a doctor.
FLORINDO. No use going for the doctor. Signor Zanetto is dead.
PROFESSOR. Dead?
BRIGHELLA. Dead! [Oh, the poor fellow!]
COLOMBINA. Poor Signor Zanetto dead?
ROSAURA. *(Coming out of the house.)* Please, father, may I come out on the street? I heard someone say that Signor Zanetto is dead; is it true?
PROFESSOR. Only too true. Look at him, the poor man.
BEATRICE. *(Coming in.)* Oh, God! What am I seeing? My darling is dead! My life, my soul!
ARLECCHINO. *(Coming in from the opposite direction.)* What's this? Signor Zanetto asleep on the street?
BRIGHELLA. Asleep forever! The poor unlucky man is dead.
ARLECCHINO. Well, that's that. Back to Bergamo for me.
PROFESSOR. We can't leave him out here like this. Let's carry him into the inn.
ROSAURA. Oh, I feel so miserable and sad.
COLOMBINA. Poor girl! You've become a widow without ever getting married. *(Aside.)* Though it cheers me up to see her so miserable.
PROFESSOR. *(Lifting ZANETTO.)* Brighella, help me bring him to the inn.
BRIGHELLA. *(Kneeling and lifting one end of body; ARLECCHINO takes the other.)* Come on, Arlecchino, lend a hand here. The poor man, it's the last job we'll ever do for him. [*(To BEATRICE'S SERVANT.)* You too.]
BEATRICE. Unhappy Beatrice! What will I do now?
FLORINDO. *(Softly, to her, gently taking her hand.)* If your Tonino is dead, then may Florindo have some hope?

BEATRICE. *(Snatching back her hand.)* I will hate you for all eternity.

ARLECCHINO. *(As they bring body into inn, having some trouble at doorway.)* Come on, friend, carry him gently, careful, even if he's dead, don't bang his head against the wall.

(ARLECCHINO, BRIGHELLA, [and the SERVANT] carry ZANETTO into the inn. NOTE: In John Rando's production, the PORTER appeared at the inn door to help them. In the confusion, a pair of prop mannequin legs, costumed like TONINO/ZANETTO's legs, are left visibly sticking out of the open inn door, as if the body were still there.)

ROSAURA. My soul is in torment.
BEATRICE. What horrible traitor could have done this?
PROFESSOR. What brought on his death?
FLORINDO. I suspect that he was poisoned.
PROFESSOR. Who would do such a thing?
FLORINDO. I don't know. But I have a good reason to believe it.
ROSAURA. We must find every clue we can, to punish whoever caused the poor man's death.
TONINO. *(Coming in suddenly to their utter astonishment.)* What's this, my Beatrice —
PROFESSOR. *(Reeling.)* Look!
BRIGHELLA. *(Likewise.)* It's Signor Zanetto's ghost!
ROSAURA & BEATRICE. No, he's alive!

(All look at each other in astonishment and shock, mixed with fright.)

ARLECCHINO. *(Coming out of the inn [with BEATRICE's SERVANT], flattens himself against door and does double take, looking back and forth from the corpse to TONINO.)* What am I seeing! I've gone crazy!
TONINO. What is all this? What's going on? [Why are you all so astonished?]
PROFESSOR. *(Tiptoeing over and gently pinching his arm.)* Signor Zanetto, are you really alive?

THE VENETIAN TWINS

TONINO. Thank God, I am.
PROFESSOR. But how was it we saw you dead at our feet not a minute ago?
TONINO. It's a flat lie. I just got here.
BRIGHELLA. What is going on here?
ARLECCHINO. Wait, wait. *(Takes two steps toward TONINO, then goes back to inn door and looks in.)* Oh, beautiful! He's half dead and half alive! Help, help!

(ARLECCHINO runs off screaming, "half dead and half alive" etc. Everyone watches in silence.)

BRIGHELLA. Hold it, hold it. *(Does as ARLECCHINO just did.)* It's a miracle! Dead in there and alive out here!

(BRIGHELLA goes to opposite side of stage from inn door, avoiding TONINO.)

PROFESSOR. I want to see too. *(Same business, except he goes straight to TONINO.)* Signor Zanetto, who is that other Signor Zanetto in there?
TONINO. Patience, my friends, patience. I'll explain everything. Just let me go in there for a minute. [I'll be right back.]

(TONINO goes into the inn. [The corpse disappears as if he has carried it to some more fitting place.] ARLECCHINO comes back during next two lines, watching along with everyone else.)

ROSAURA. I thank God that Signor Zanetto is still alive.
BEATRICE. Though Tonino's been unfaithful to me, I still wish him life.
TONINO. *(Coming out of the inn, shocked and sad.)* Now I see! I understand everything at last — but too late. The man who is lying dead in there is my twin brother, Zanetto.
PROFESSOR. But then who are you?
TONINO. I am Tonino Bisognosi, poor Zanetto's Venetian twin.
ROSAURA. What am I hearing?

PROFESSOR. What kind of absurd nonsense is this?
BEATRICE. Then — you are my love!

(BEATRICE runs to TONINO.)

TONINO. Yes, I'm yours. But why did you tear up my letter, and call me all those names? [Why did you treat me that way?]
BEATRICE. Why did you say you were giving me up? And then why did you make love to Miss Rosaura?
TONINO. Steady, my dear, steady. The resemblance between me and my brother has caused a lot of confusion. I am yours, you are mine, and that's the whole story.
ROSAURA. But, Signor Zanetto, what about the promises you made to me?
TONINO. I'm not Zanetto. And I can't marry you.
PROFESSOR. Whether you're Tonino or Zanetto, if you're not too grand to marry into my family, my daughter can still be yours. *(Aside.)* Now that he's the sole heir, he'll be even richer than his brother was.
TONINO. Very well, I'm ready to marry your daughter.
BEATRICE. Tonino!

(Behind his back, out of PROFESSOR'S line of vision, TONINO signals to her not to worry.)

PROFESSOR. Fine, then I give you her hand. *(Moving ROSAURA toward him.)*
TONINO. *(As he is about to take ROSAURA's hand.)* But — where is your daughter?
PROFESSOR. Right here.
TONINO. Go on, you amaze me. This isn't your daughter.
PROFESSOR. What? What are you saying?
TONINO. You see, I know everything. I know about the pilgrim. [I know the whole story.]
PROFESSOR. *(To COLOMBINA.)* You chatterbox, I'm furious at you.
COLOMBINA. Oh, now look, I didn't say anything —

THE VENETIAN TWINS

TONINO. But tell me, Professor, the locket that you found in the baby's clothes, do you still have it?

PROFESSOR. *(Aside.)* He even knows all about the locket! *(To TONINO.)* You mean the one with the double portrait?

TONINO. Yes, a portrait of two little boys.

PROFESSOR. Here, look at it. Is this what you mean?

TONINO. Yes[, that's it]. *(Aside.)* My father had it made when Zanetto and I were born.

PROFESSOR. Since you know everything, I admit it. Rosaura is not my daughter. She's a foundling, discovered by a pilgrim on his way to Rome, in the foothills of Caldiera, between here and Vicenza. The pilgrim said he found her on the ground, alone and abandoned in her cradle, after highway robbers had looted and killed everyone riding in the coach that carried her. I begged him to leave her with me, and I've always raised her to believe she was my own daughter.

TONINO. She is my sister Flaminia, whom my poor mother was taking to Bergamo, [where she wanted to visit my brother Zanetto, and leave Flaminia, like him,] to be raised by my rich uncle Stefanello. They were attacked near Caldiera[, and my mother, along with everyone else in the coach, was killed]. But by some miracle it seems the baby was left alone, and survived.

ROSAURA. *(To TONINO.)* Now I understand the love I feel for you. You're my family and my own blood.

TONINO. And that's exactly why I felt drawn to you.

BEATRICE. So there seems to be no way Tonino can marry Miss Rosaura.

FLORINDO. *(Aside.)* And I've lost all hope of marrying Miss Beatrice.

TONINO. *(To ROSAURA.)* And now I understand the mix-up about the two letters and the friendly way you treated me. *(To PROFESSOR.)* And the terrible way I misinterpreted the poor Professor's behavior.

PROFESSOR. Yes, you've ruined me!

TONINO. How so?

PROFESSOR. You see, my brother left me thirty thousand ducats, on condition that I use it to bring up my daughter, Rosaura, the one child of my marriage. But the child died, and I would have lost the inheritance; by the terms of the will, it would have gone to my nephew instead. I needed a little girl in order not to lose all that money, so I looked for an orphan girl to replace my dead Rosaura. This child came to my hands, and with the help of the nursemaid, Colombina's mother, I was able to work things out. But now that all is revealed, my nephew can still demand the inheritance, with interest, which after all these years would be a sum large enough to destroy me.

TONINO. But who is your nephew?

PROFESSOR. A certain Lelio[, my sister's son].

TONINO. That swaggering cartoon who goes around pretending to be a count and a marquis?

PROFESSOR. Yes, that's the one.

TONINO. Look, here he comes now. Let me deal with him, and don't worry about a thing.

(All clear aside as LELIO comes in, waving a battle ax.)

LELIO. Stop, stop, all of you! I am a desperate man!

TONINO. Be strong, Master Lelio. There is no cure for you. Beatrice will be my wife.

LELIO. I will turn hell upside down! I will ravage the earth!

TONINO. But why would you want to do all that?

LELIO. Because I'm desperate!

TONINO. I have a cure for your despair.

LELIO. What is it?

TONINO. Marry your cousin Rosaura, with a dowry of fifteen thousand ducats, and as much again after the Professor's death.

LELIO. Thirty thousand ducats for a dowry? I like the concept.

TONINO. And do you like the girl?

LELIO. Who doesn't like the girl? Thirty thousand ducats make a great deal of beauty.

TONINO. Then it's done, [and we'll settle the details later. It's not proper to discuss them in the street]. Let's go in the house and we'll arrange everything. Beatrice will be mine, Rosaura will marry Lelio. *(Too ROSAURA.)* If that's all right with you?

ROSAURA. I'll do whatever my father thinks is right.

THE VENETIAN TWINS 93

PROFESSOR. Good girl! You've brought me back to life. Dear Signor Tonino, I'm very much in your debt. But let's go and draw up the agreement, while it's all fresh in our minds.

(The PROFESSOR starts moving toward his house, with ROSAURA under his wing.)

TONINO. This way everyone will be happy.
FLORINDO. Except for me. I'm so miserable at the way I betrayed our friendship.
TONINO. You should be ashamed; you did the most terrible thing a man can do. But I forgive you, because you were in love; and the remorse you feel makes me glad to have you as my friend again. *(Offers his hand.)*
FLORINDO. I don't deserve your generosity, but I accept it, *(Grasping his hand.)* and I swear I'll be a faithful friend from now on.
PANCRAZIO. *(Coming in.)* What can I be seeing? Zanetto's not dead? Didn't he drink the poison? [I was an idiot to think he'd do it.]
PROFESSOR. Signor Pancrazio, come quickly. We have some wonderful news.
PANCRAZIO. If you'll forgive me for a moment. *(Taking TONINO aside, softly.)* Tell me, did you drink it?
TONINO. Drink? Are you saying I'm drunk?
PANCRAZIO. No, I mean did you drink the medicine I gave you?
TONINO. *(Aside.)* Hold on, I think this may explain everything. *(To PANCRAZIO.)* No, no, I decided not to drink it just yet.
PANCRAZIO. But then, if the women torment you, how will you endure it?
TONINO. But how can I avoid it?
PANCRAZIO. As soon as you've drunk the powder, you'll be free.
TONINO. But how should I drink it?
PANCRAZIO. You know! In the wine. [You saw me put the powder in the wine, didn't you? You still have the goblet, I hope.]
TONINO. *(Aside.)* [A goblet of] wine with powder in it. Now I see. *(To PANCRAZIO, loudly, backing away from him as everyone*

THE VENETIAN TWINS

else turns to stare at them.) You evil scoundrel, [you whited sepulcher,] you god-damned two-faced hypocrite! You, you're the one who murdered my brother. [Yes, he drank your medicine, he went to the next world in agony, because of you.] I'm not Zanetto, I'm Tonino. We were identical twins[, and our resemblance has trapped you]. Now tell me, you snake, you murderer, you traitor, why did you kill him? Why did you murder my brother?

PANCRAZIO. [You amaze me. None of that happened.] I never did any such thing. I have a reputation. [I would be incapable of acting that way.]

TONINO. Then why did you ask me if I'd drunk your medicine? [If I wanted to be free of women?]

PANCRAZIO. I only meant — that you should drink — to your wedding, to celebrate your marriage.

TONINO. Then why are you so confused? Monster, murderer[, fiend]!

PANCRAZIO. Oh, ye gods! Can I hear all this and not die?

PROFESSOR. But Signor Pancrazio is the soul of honor. I can swear to that myself.

FLORINDO. But I found a goblet of wine near Zanetto's body, and it was all cloudy, like something had been mixed in it.

COLOMBINA. And Signor Pancrazio came into the house a little while ago and took a goblet of wine, when he thought no one was looking.

FLORINDO. Let's see if it's the same one.

TONINO. If you killed him, God have mercy on you. [And what did you do with the jewels?

PANCRAZIO. The judge is holding them.

TONINO. Good, then at least there's a chance of getting them back.]

FLORINDO. *(Showing goblet.)* This is the wine that killed Zanetto.

COLOMBINA. And that's the same goblet Signor Pancrazio took from the house.

TONINO. Is it?

PANCRAZIO. It is.

TONINO. Then you did poison him.

THE VENETIAN TWINS

PANCRAZIO. It's not true. I'm a gentleman. I'll prove to you that I'm innocent. Give me that wine.
FLORINDO. Here.
PANCRAZIO. See, I'm drinking it.

(PANCRAZIO drinks. BEATRICE grabs TONINO in horror. PANCRAZIO shows FLORINDO that goblet is now empty.)

PROFESSOR. See! I told you. Signor Pancrazio could never do such a terrible thing.
TONINO. *(Aside.)* It can't be poison if he's drinking it.
COLOMBINO. *(Aside.)* If only it could be poison.
TONINO. Oh. God! Look at his eyes! It's gotten to him!
PANCRAZIO. *(Drops goblet, feeling the effects of the poison.)* Friends, I'm dead, there's no antidote. I'll tell you everything, I'm at the end. *(Turning to TONINO.)* I loved Rosaura, and I couldn't stand to see her marry anyone else. I poisoned that poor fellow to get rid of my rival. *(Staggers slightly; those he staggers toward back away.)* Oh, God, I can't go on. I'm dying, I'm dying a scoundrel's death. My life was the same; my goodness was all a pose, a fraud. *(Backs up against wall, pulling himself together.)* Let me be a lesson to you, never believe people who set themselves up as models of virtue. The most wicked scoundrels of all are those who pretend to be good, and aren't. Goodbye, my friends. I shall die in despair.

(PANCRAZIO draws himself up to his full height and goes out with dignity, staggering slightly. We hear a thud offstage. Silence for one instant.)

COLOMBINA. I always told you he was a sneak.
TONINO. He's even cheated the executioner. My poor brother! [I'm so unhappy.] Dear sister, my consolation is that I've found you, [but I hate to think of poor Zanetto dying like that].
ROSAURA. I'm as sad as you are, but we have to bear it with patience.
PROFESSOR. Come, let's go in the house.
TONINO. If you don't mind, I'll bring in my fiancée. *(Taking*

THE VENETIAN TWINS

BEATRICE's hand.)
    LELIO. *(Giving ROSAURA his arm.)* And I'll escort my goddess.
    PROFESSOR. Come in, all of you, to witness the agreements we're drawing up. *(Aside.)* Let's get the money settled, that's all I want.

(The PROFESSOR pauses in doorway as TONINO stops and comes downstage to look back at the corpse in the inn door.)

    TONINO. My brother must be buried in Venice; I'll have to go back there to arrange it. [If he had lived, he would have gone back to Caldiera with me to catch those bandits; but I'll gladly do that myself.] Thanks to my good luck, I've found a sister and a wife, in spite of his terrible death, and in spite of all the incredible mix-ups that happened — and all in one day! — to THE VENETIAN TWINS.

(CONSTABLE, who has entered with casket of jewels on "Thanks to my good luck," comes forward after "his terrible death" and hands jewels to TONINO, who hands them to ROSAURA, and embraces BEATRICE while finishing speech. ROSAURA and LELIO gloat over jewels, PROFESSOR hovering in background; ARLECCHINO and COLOMBINA embrace; BRIGHELLA watches, beaming, from doorway; FLORINDO, disconsolate, from inn door.)

CURTAIN

ABOUT THE AUTHOR

CARLO GOLDONI (1707-1793) was acclaimed in his own time as one of the world's great masters of comic playwriting, and still holds his high rank today, more than two centuries after his death. At least three of his plays — *The Servant of Two Masters*, *La Locandiera* (sometimes called *Mirandolina* in English), and *The Venetian Twins* — are often performed in all Western countries. In Italy, at least ten other Goldoni plays are part of the standard repertoire. He also wrote opera libretti, and his plays provided the source for many more, inspiring composers from Piccinni and Haydn to Wolf-Ferrari and Malipiero, so that his work survives on recordings, in opera houses, and in concert halls as well as in the theatre. Goldoni works that were once obscure, like *Il Campiello*, *Le barufe Chiozzotte*, and the *Villeggiatura* or "Vacation" trilogy, are now well-known on the world's stages.

From a middle-class Venetian family, Goldoni was intended by his parents to be a lawyer, but his fascination with the theatre interrupted his legal studies time and again. Though he finally received his law degree from the University of Padua in 1731, he never practiced, instead giving all his energy to playwriting. In his first comedies, he followed what was then the standard pattern for Italian theatre troupes, writing *soggetti* (scenarios) on which the actors would improvise, with only key roles or the dialogue of pivotal scenes written out in full. *The Venetian Twins* (1746) was one of the first plays with which he was able to persuade the entire cast to speak the lines as written; its sensational popularity in Venice permanently altered the Italian theatre's anti-literary stance.

Goldoni followed up this triumph with a series of masterworks and near-masterworks in which he explored, with innovative realism and sparkling wit, every area of Venice, every class, and every profession. Aside from the plays already mentioned, *The Liar*, *The Fan*, *The Boors*, *The Coffeehouse*, *The Clever Widow*, and *The New Home* are among those that have remained popular with Italian audiences. He extended his reforms into comic opera with his libretti, bringing the form a new coherence and turning it towards the whole variety of contemporary life. In a century when Italian was universally viewed as the language of learning and high culture, his works quickly spread across Europe, and with them his reputation.

In Venice itself, however, his theatrical reforms had provoked a backlash among those who clung to the old improvised tradition, including the influential critic and poet, Count Carlo Gozzi. Gozzi proved his point, in the early 1760s, by scoring enormous successes with a series of fairytale plays that were bare skeletons for improvisation and spectacle. As the most vocal leader of the party that sought to remove Goldoni's innovations, Gozzi may or may not also have been responsible for the more reprehensible tactics — including threats on Goldoni's life and the spreading of scurrilous gossip about him — that finally made the great playwright weary of the struggle.

To escape Venice and its annoyances, Goldoni accepted a position as writer in residence to the Théâtre Italien of Paris, where he found himself fighting the same artistic battles all over again. His prestige was such, however, that in 1762 he was appointed Italian tutor to the children of King Louis XV, and he spent the next few decades in Paris, living on a meager royal stipend, continuing to turn out plays and libretti. Chronic shortness of money made him compose his unreliable but highly entertaining *Memoirs* in French, which by the late 1770s he had mastered sufficiently to write plays in that language. One result was a commission from the *Comédie-Française*, to create a new comedy for their contribution to the wedding celebrations of the future Louis XVI and the Austrian princess Marie Antoinette — who, familiar with Goldoni's work from Vienna, had specially requested a performance of a play by him. Voltaire declared the result, *Le bourru bienfaisant* (*The Kind-Hearted Curmudgeon*) to be the best comedy written in French since Molière. The play became immensely popular, but, because of its monarchist associations, was withdrawn from the repertoire after the Revolution; the loss of its royalties reduced Goldoni to destitution. His standing among the literate was so high, however, that even his links with the former regime did not keep the new National Assembly from voting to grant him a pension, which he did not live to receive; it was transferred to his widow and children by unanimous vote of the Assembly, a final instance of the high esteem in which he was held.

ABOUT THE TRANSLATOR

MICHAEL FEINGOLD is a graduate of Columbia University, where he majored in Comparative Literature, and the Yale School of Drama, where he received an MFA in Dramatic Literature and Criticism, going on to become the first Literary Manager of the newly founded Yale Repertory Theatre, a post he held from 1970 to 1976. He subsequently served as Literary Director of the Guthrie Theatre in Minneapolis and the American Repertory Theatre in Cambridge, Mass. His numerous translations for these and other resident theatres include works by Ibsen, Molière, Diderot, Gerhart Hauptmann, and Max Frisch, as well as all the major music-theatre collaborations of Bertolt Brecht and Kurt Weill. His versions of *Happy End* (available from Samuel French) and *The Threepenny Opera*, both seen on Broadway, are now the standard ones authorized by the Kurt Weill Foundation. *Happy End* received Tony Award nominations for Best Book and Lyrics. His translation of Schiller's *Mary Stuart*, commissioned by San Francisco's American Conservatory Theatre, was received with acclaim both there and at Boston's Huntington Theatre, where its production received the Elliot Norton Award for Best Production by a Resident Theatre.

Off Broadway, his lyrics have been heard in *Berlin to Broadway with Kurt Weill*, and he has translated two contemporary French plays, Copi's *Grand Finale* and Picq's *Case of Kaspar Mayer*, for Ubu Rep. His association with Off-Broadway's Pearl Theatre, which began with *The Venetian Twins*, has gone on to include translations of Scribe's *When Ladies Battle*, Beaumarchais' *Barber of Seville*, Goldoni's *Mirandolina*, and Regnard's *A Will of His Own*.

Michael's opera translations include Donizetti's *Viva la Mamma* and Offenbach's *La Perichole* for San Francisco Opera, and Penderecki's *The Black Mask* for its American premiere at Santa Fe Opera. His translation of Weill's *Mahagonny*, originally produced by the Yale Rep, was broadcast from Chicago's Lyric Opera in 1999 as part of the celebration of the Kurt Weill Centennial. Michael's new stage book for Cole Porter's *Aladdin* has been produced in four Asian cities by National Touring Musicals. He regularly teaches criticism for the Eugene O'Neill Center's National Critics Institute, and has also taught in the Dramatic Writing Program at NYU's Tisch School of the Arts, and in the Theatre Program at Columbia University's Hammersteiin Center for the Arts. His nontheatrical translations include tests by Ibsen, Rimbaud, and Kafka for the limited-edition artists' books of Vincent FitzGerald & Company, described by many critics as "the most beautiful books in the world." He wrote the introduction to the Lambda Award-winning anthology *The Way We Live Now: American Plays and the AIDS Crisis* (TCG Publications), and is the editor of many anthologies, most recently *Grove New American Theater* (Grove Press).

Despite all his work in the theatre, however, Michael is best known as the chief theater critic of New York's weekly newspaper, *The Village Voice*, where he has written major reviews and essays on theater for the past thirty years. As a critic, he has been a Pulitzer Prize finalist, a Geoge Jean Nathan Award winner, and a Senior Fellow of the National Arts Journalism Program.

ABOUT *COMMEDIA DELL'ARTE*

The phrase literally means "professional theatre." It differentiates actors trained to do their work with skill ("*arte*") from the wealthy folk who did it only out of love, and hence were "*amatori*" — the source of our word "amateurs." The phrase dates from the 15th century, when troupes of strolling players crisscrossed Italy, often spilling over into the rest of southern Europe, playing pieces of various kinds — the repertoire included tragedies, farces, topical dramas, and fairy-tale-like fantasies — that were improvised *a soggetto*: that is, on a scenario posted backstage for each day's performance.

This does not mean that *commedia* performers had no idea what they were going to say when they made their entrance. As the word "*arte*" implies, theirs was an elaborate and highly skilled art, evolved over years of experience. The extremely conventionalized stories (some are thought to have descended from the ancient Roman farces of Plautus and Terence) were played out by a set of stock characters, each equipped with his or her own set of stock phrases, reactions, and bits of physical business, all carefully rehearsed in advance. The young lovers, singly or in duet, spoke high-flown *concetti* — elaborate metaphors, drawn from Renaissance poetry, describing their passion or their loved one's beauty. The comedians included parodies of these filigreed rhapsodies among their *lazzi*, sequences of back-and-forth wordplay or physical slapstick that were the equivalent of our century's vaudeville routines or "shtick." Sustaining a single role from play to play, each actor constantly looked for and worked out new "bits" that could be polished and added to the character's repertory of phrases and gestures; they noted these down in the *zibaldone*, or notebook, that every *commedia* performer carried, a treasured possession to be passed on to his or her successor in the role, often a family member.

Commedia characters, like those in the Roman farces, wore masks, though not the Roman kind, which had had resonators of some organic substance built into the mouth area. Lacking this technique (lost with the decline of ancient Roman civilization), and playing in town squares or torch-lit palace ballrooms rather than vast arenas, *commedia* actors cultivated their natural voices, using masks that covered the upper half of the face and kept the mouth free, while the aristocratic young lovers, roles in which freshness and good looks were important assets, performed unmasked. Decades of catering to local preferences wherever they toured taught the troupes to associate each of the stock characters with the dialect and manners of a specific region. The Dottore, or professor, usually a lawyer who tried to impress the others with his big words, was from Bologna, where the University was renowned for its legal training; he traditionally wore an academic gown. Pantalone, the greedy and lecherous old merchant, was associated with the thriving mercantile center of Venice, and wore the baggy striped trousers (hence "pantaloons") once fashionable in that city. The comic servants, malicious, swarthy Brighella and naive, pale-faced Arlecchino, were associated with the peasants of the Bergamo countryside. There were many variants of each type, with variant names; the most popular actors prided themselves on the individuality of their creations. The rich performing tradition absorbed many styles and could take on many forms, becoming crude or refined, satiric or fantastical, hearty or bitter and grotesque, as the artists assembled for each troupe saw fit.

By the late 18th century, however, theatre-going had regularized, in Italy as elsewhere, with the growth of the mercantile class. Most towns had indoor theatres where touring companies could appear; the increasing popularity of opera gave the spoken theatre increasingly strong competition. Falling back on the stalest routines and the most obvious jokes, the *commedia* companies had reduced themselves to a dreary level comparable to that of television sitcoms. Goldoni's reforms, with their new insistence on realistic observation and the value of the playwright's art, changed all that. After him there was no turning back, despite the temporary craze for Gozzi's return to the fairytale-spectacle side of the genre: The old *commedia dell'arte* was gone, but in its place was an Italian dramatic literature that could stand with the drama of England, France, and Germany. Though in the 19th century it would be overshadowed by the triumph of Italian romantic opera, the theatre Goldoni made out of the *commedia* would ultimately become the theatre of Duse and the realist playwrights, of Pirandello, of Eduardo de Filippo and Dario Fo. Without Goldoni, it might have remained a theatre of scenarios and ephemeral recollections, or have disappeared entirely.

THE VENETIAN TWINS

THE SET

The basic set is the street, with the inn door stage right and the front door of the Professor's house stage left. At the Pearl, there were additional exits upstage and downstage of each. In addition, Robert Joel Schwartz's set put a wooden picket fence upstage (backed by a drop of similar buildings in the distance), with a large gap in the center, so that characters could also exit upstage left and right behind the fence. The Professor's house has a practical upstairs window.

For the interiors, the center area of the street was blocked from view by a four-panel screen, decorated 18th-century style. In front of this, only the necessary furniture was brought on: A dressing table and low-backed seat for Rosaura's room; a couch and an end table with a chessboard for the parlor.

A WORD ABOUT PANCRAZIO

When not self-explanatory, the behavior of most of the characters in this play can be understood in terms of their *commedia dell'arte* archetypes, on which volumes of material exist. The exception is Pancrazio, for whom the commedia offers no exact antecedent, though the hypocrite as a figure in drama is hardly new. One obvious source for the character is Molière's *Tartuffe*, a play Goldoni certainly knew and undoubtedly admired, but Pancrazio equally owes a good deal to observation from life, and to the Italian folktale tradition, memorialized in Renaissance story collections like Boccacio's *Decameron*, in which the lecherous and falsely pious priest is a recurring figure. Like Molière, Goldoni could not make his hypocrite a functionary of the established Church without running into censorship trouble, but he sailed as close to the edge of the permissible as he dared. Given the practices carried on in our own time in the name of religion, groups wishing to take this character a step closer to the edge can feel sure that they have the translator's blessing, if not the original author's. I should add that, every time I showed up at the Pearl's performances, at least one customer in the lobby would invariably ask me if I had interpolated Pancrazio's final speech as a dig at the religious right. It is identical, almost word for word, to Goldoni's original.

THE CASKET OF JEWELS

In John Rando's production, the audience never saw what was in the casket, but a light inside it cast an eerie glow on whoever opened the casket, and an eerie tremolo underscored the event until the casket was shut. Obviously, this is not an invitation to clutter the script with gag embroidery, but a clever director can make such a convention, once set up, both add to the comedy of the show and heighten its dramatic tension. It isn't the eerie lighting and music cues, of course; it's how the actors play to them.